Johnson After Three Centuries:

New Light on Texts and Contexts

T0327285

Edited by
Thomas A. Horrocks
and
Howard D. Weinbrot

HOUGHTON LIBRARY OF THE HARVARD COLLEGE LIBRARY 2011

Distributed by Harvard University Press
Cambridge, Massachusetts and London, England

A Special Issue of the *Harvard Library Bulletin*
Volume 20: Numbers 3-4

HARVARD LIBRARY BULLETIN
VOLUME 20: NUMBERS 3-4 (FALL-WINTER 2009)
PUBLISHED JUNE 2011
ISSN 0017-8136

Editor	*Coordinating Editor*
William P. Stoneman	Dennis C. Marnon

The Harvard Library Bulletin *is published quarterly by Houghton Library of the Harvard College Library. Annual subscription $35 (U.S., Canada, and Mexico), $41 (foreign); single issue $15.*

Editorial correspondence should be addressed to William P. Stoneman, Houghton Library, Harvard University, Cambridge, MA 02138, email stoneman@fas.harvard.edu; claims and subscription inquiries should be addressed to Monique Duhaime, Houghton Library, Harvard University, Cambridge, MA 02138, email duhaime@fas.harvard.edu.

Publication of the Bulletin *is made possible by a bequest from George L. Lincoln '95, by a fund established in memory of William A. Jackson, and by the Endowment Fund for the Donald & Mary Hyde Collection of Dr. Samuel Johnson.*

The paper used in this publication meets the minimum requirements of the American National Standard for Information Sciences—Permanence of Paper for Printed Materials, ANSI z39.49-1984.

Contents

Preface

THIS SPECIAL ISSUE OF THE *HARVARD LIBRARY BULLETIN* examines several aspects of Samuel Johnson's career through fresh perspectives and original interpretations by some of the best-known and widely-respected scholars of our time. Four of the five essays presented here were delivered at "Johnson at 300," a symposium sponsored by Houghton Library and held at Harvard University on August 27–29, 2009, and one was presented before the annual dinner of The Johnsonians, held at the university in conjunction with the symposium. Also included is a bibliography of works on Johnson's *Dictionary* published from 1955 to 2009, the tercentenary year of Johnson's birth.

Harvard University was an appropriate location to celebrate the Johnson tercentenary, and it is fitting that the *Harvard Library Bulletin* serves as a venue for the latest in Johnson scholarship. As the repository of the Donald & Mary Hyde Collection of Dr. Samuel Johnson, received in 2004 as a bequest of Mary Hyde Eccles, Harvard's Houghton Library is one of the world's premier centers for the study of eighteenth-century literature in general and of Samuel Johnson and his circle in particular.

I would like to acknowledge those individuals who in various ways made this publication possible. First of all, I would like to thank my co-editor, Howard Weinbrot, for bringing his deep knowledge of Johnson and of the eighteenth century to the task of producing this issue and contributing an insightful Introduction, and each of the contributors for providing the edifying and enlightening content. My Houghton colleagues, William Stoneman, Florence Fearrington Librarian of Houghton Library and Editor of the *Harvard Library Bulletin*, and Dennis Marnon, Coordinating Editor, deserve special thanks for their assistance in seeing this publication through the editing process. I also want to thank Duncan Todd for designing this publication and Paul Adams of the Harvard University Press for his efforts concerning the distribution of this special double issue of the *Harvard Library Bulletin*. Support for the publication of this double issue of the *Harvard Library Bulletin* is provided by the Endowment Fund for the Donald & Mary Hyde Collection of Dr. Samuel Johnson.

Thomas A. Horrocks

Introduction

Samuel Johnson After Three Hundred Years, and Beyond

Howard D. Weinbrot

WE NOW HAVE EXPERIENCED SOME THREE HUNDRED YEARS of Johnsonian biography, study, discussion, and friendly squabbles over meaning. We also have experienced historical, political, formal, Freudian, Marxist, colonial, imperial, lexicographic, and many other kinds of analyses of his major and minor works. Readers may legitimately ask, What more there is to learn about Samuel Johnson? The distinguished Johnsonians in the following essays offer some tentative answers to that question. They presented their papers at the Houghton Library's remarkable "Johnson at 300" symposium on August 27–29, 2009. Professor James Engell delivered his paper just prior to the appended annual dinner meeting of the Johnsonians.[1]

1.

The contributors range across many aspects of Johnson's career and achievement. Nicholas Hudson's "Johnson and Revolution" carefully considers Johnson's comments on the Revolution of 1688, locates these within his age's political attitudes, and assesses his contribution to the concept of "revolution." In so doing, Hudson finds fluidity within the concepts of Whig and Tory, whose values change over time. Some Whigs thought James II's forced abdication a restoration of the ancient constitution. More radical Whigs thought it a timid reform that should have gone much further. Tories gradually moved away from Jacobite principles like passive obedience and divine right. They settled for a strong monarch whom they hoped to have found in George III, and whom they defended from radicals' attacks. Within these contexts, if Johnson was at

[1]   For a discussion of the Houghton symposium and the Johnsonian dinner, see J. T. Scanlan, "The Houghton Library Symposium," *Johnsonian News Letter* 61 (2010): 20–23. The same number includes memorials of the Pembroke College, Oxford, and Lichfield celebrations during the handsome three-week birthday party in the months around Johnson's birth, September 18, 1709, new style.

all "Jacobite" it was more likely to have been in his later than in his early years, and associated with the continuity of George III's part in the constitution rather than James II's. This need for a powerful, constitutional, royal presence probably would have put Johnson on Edmund Burke's side regarding the French Revolution, in which Burke in effect repudiated his criticisms of the throne in the 1770s.

James Basker's "Johnson and Slavery" has three important functions. It demonstrates Johnson's antipathy to slavery and the ways in which it manifested itself in his life, writings, and relationship with his black servant and surrogate son Francis Barber. It distinguishes between Johnson's views and Boswell's, who was both indifferent to the plight of slaves and unsympathetic to critics of slavery like Johnson. It also recovers elements of what Basker calls "the story Boswell never told"—namely, the legal brief Johnson wrote on behalf of the slave Joseph Knight that Boswell claimed to have misplaced and that he reproduced only as a difficult-to-find addendum to the *Life of Johnson*'s second edition. Basker also considers Johnson's twenty-five year membership in Bray's Associates, a charity that funded schools for black children in the slave colonies. We have a new perspective not only on Johnson's attitude toward racial slavery, but also on the ways in which Boswell, among other biographers, may have obscured that morally urgent aspect of Johnson's mind and art.

James Engell's "Johnson on Blackmore, Pope, Shakespeare—and Johnson" adds new insights regarding the *Lives of the Poets* in general and the often ignored "Life of Blackmore" in particular. Johnson both insisted that Blackmore be included and quoted liberally from his works. Johnson regularly contrasts Blackmore's virtuous life which he praises and, *Creation* excepted, his poetry which he laments. Pope was personally malignant but a great poet. Blackmore was personally virtuous but a mediocre poet. This aspect of the *Lives* represents one of Johnson's insufficiently acknowledged and perhaps disturbing critical and psychological insights: the relationship between literary genius and moral virtue may be more than uncertain.

Allen Reddick's "Vindicating Milton: Poetic Misprision in Johnson's *Dictionary of the English Language*" is one of this volume's three contributions to the study of the 1755 *Dictionary*. Reddick carefully navigates through what he regards as Scylla and Charybdis readings of Johnson's illustrative quotations. In his judgment, they neither reflect Johnson's own considered opinions on all matters, nor are meaningless evocations of words designed only to clarify usage. Nonetheless, in some cases the illustrative quotations suggest certain patterns. His essay attempts to trace the ways in which Johnson uses and in some cases misuses Milton's poetry. These may imply Johnson's attitudes towards Milton and political and literary history. Certain quotations may perhaps seem ironic or mock-heroic at Milton's expense. Reddick argues that the *Dictionary* participates in the transformation of Milton from the once republican and dangerous political activist to the great epic poet he had become in the national canon. Johnson also uses one of Pope's key lines to suggest a critique of Milton.

Jack Lynch's "Modes of Definition in Johnson and His Contemporaries" hopes to begin resolution of a paradox in studies of Johnson's lexicography: his definitions are the least examined element of that great work. Lynch compares and contrasts Johnson's mode of proceeding with those by nine other English lexicographers from Robert Cawdrey (1604) to Charles Richardson (1818–1837). Examining the frequency of nine modes of definitions in Johnson's *Dictionary* and those other works from the early seventeenth to the mid-nineteenth centuries makes it possible to see the extent of Johnson's originality in defining English words. Johnson's methods generally were consistent with those of the other lexicographers, though he makes greater use of the antonym than they do. He also shows less interest in the genus-differentiae style of definition, in which a word is defined by giving its kind and the differences from others of its kind. Lynch's tentative conclusions suggest new ways further to examine Johnson's definitions in his book of definitions.

Lynch also has assembled an important bibliography of studies that focus on Johnson's *Dictionary* from the publication of James H. Sledd and Gwin J. Kolb's seminal *Dr. Johnson's Dictionary: Essays in the Biography of a Book* (1955) to 2009, the Johnson 300 year and the varied celebrations in his honor. Johnson's *Dictionary* indeed is among the single most analyzed texts in the English language. As Lynch's bibliography shows, it has been discussed in at least eight countries beyond those for which English is the native language.

We have, then, new light on Johnson's general view of monarchy, politics, civil rights, and human freedom. We see how the biography of a minor poet reflects Johnson's larger concept of the tenuous relationship between a good life and good art. We also see two of his lexical methods: how to define words, and how to use illustrative quotations. These sometimes altered quotations may have reflected, if not influenced, Milton's changing reputation from regicide to transcendent epic poet. The substantial bibliography of *Dictionary* studies denotes its importance in the history of the English language and of lexicography in general.

2.

The wealth of these and other Johnsonian interventions suggests that the more we learn the more we need to learn. Few of us, for example, knew that in 2005, the *Dictionary*'s 250th anniversary, the Church of England anointed Johnson as a minor saint. December 13 in the *Book of Common Worship* now includes "Samuel Johnson, Moralist, 1784." That month of course includes exalted religious company and events central to Christian worship. Though I cannot gild the handsome lily of sanctification, I hope to add a little to that increasing store of knowledge about Johnson and his contexts. I briefly consider an essentially ignored commentator and journal-editor with whom Johnson was in occasional contact. I am referring to Thomas Bellamy and his *General Magazine*

Howard D. Weinbrot 3

and Impartial Review (1787–1792). Much of the *General Magazine* also is important in the history of the eighteenth-century stage, in the textual propagation of Shakespeare's plays, and, for our purposes, with discussion of Johnson's religion, publication of his sermons and prayers. These were the subject of an especially rich and packed session at the Houghton symposium.

The *General Magazine* included several items regarding Johnson, Boswell, Mrs. Piozzi, and other members of Johnson's wide circle. Bellamy was a demonstrable Johnsonophile, in part because of what seems like a psychological and almost stylistic sympathy. As he says in the *Rambler*-like "Introductory Essay" to the *General Magazine*, "Certain it is, that the miseries of millions may be attributed to those amusements which idleness never fails to throw in the way of such as have leisure to be idle" (1 [June, 1787]: 6). Thereafter, he tells readers that his *Magazine* must not have any moral impurities. It is "intended to convey, sentiments of purity and of truth" (6 [1792]: sig. A3^r). Bellamy's later *Monthly Mirror* praises Johnson's periodical essays as the lone worthy heirs of Addison and Steele, whose animation, genius, and soul had disappeared in their later imitators: Johnson carried his unparalleled "profundity of thought and subtilety of discrimination" into his *Rambler* papers.[2]

Though Bellamy himself was not profound, he played a significant if small part in the later eighteenth-century literary world. He busied himself in managing the *General Magazine* and other entrepreneurial publishing ventures. He wrote stories, a play, and poems; he engaged artists for numerous engravings and organized much of the layout for the *General Magazine*; he selected portions of Shakespeare's plays that regularly were printed with each number; and he supervised the reviews of recent publications, some of which I suspect he wrote himself.[3] Unlike Johnson's major biographers, Bellamy had no stake in Johnsonian sibling rivalries, and unlike Boswell he is able to praise Mrs. Piozzi for her contributions to Johnson's milieu. In January 1788 Bellamy reviews Mrs.

2   *The Monthly Mirror: Reflecting Men and Manners, with Strictures on Their Epitome, the Stage* 1 (1795): iv–v.

3   Bellamy's biographical details are best found in Elizabeth Sarah Villa-Real Gooch's memoir prefixed to his posthumously published *The Beggar Boy: A Novel, in Three Volumes . . . By the Late Mr. Thomas Bellamy. To which are now prefixed, Biographical Particulars of the Author* (London: Earl & Hemet, 1801). She insists that an unnamed reviewer was responsible for all of the *General Magazine*'s many reviews (1: xxii–xxiii). I am indebted to Isobel Grundy for alerting me to this work. Given the virtual congruence with the reviews' judgments and Bellamy's known beliefs regarding Johnson, it is at the least plausible that Bellamy wrote them or had a hand in them. He certainly approved of their warm praise of all matters Johnsonian. I use the shorthand of "Bellamy" as Johnson's reviewer, especially given the personal contact implicit in the reviews. *The Monthly Mirror* reviewed *The Beggar Boy* and offered two corrections to Villa-Real Gooch's account: Bellamy broke with Dibdin before, not after, the publication of his *Miscellanies*, and he received the major portion of the income from *The Monthly Mirror* for the last five years of his life. See the *Mirror* 12 (December 1801): 181–182.

Piozzi's *Letters to and from the late Samuel Johnson, LL.D.* Any information regarding that good man, he says, "must be greatly acceptable to all who know how to appreciate the value of such communication." Unfortunately, the many who criticized Mrs. Piozzi's *Anecdotes* of Johnson (1786) and Boswell's *Journal of a Tour to the Hebrides* with Johnson (1786) forgot "that nothing true can be known tending to disgrace him" (2 [January, 1788]:143). There are other remarks in defense of Mrs. Piozzi and her works, as there are of Johnson. I will focus briefly on Bellamy's, or his reviewer's, observations regarding Johnson's sermons.

John Taylor's *A Letter to Samuel Johnson, LL.D. on the subject of a Future State* (1787) responded to Johnson's remark that he would rather have a state of torment than of annihilation.[4] Taylor fears that such a view could disrupt tender minds, and he engages Johnson in posthumous discourse which he was fortunate enough not to hear in the Great Beyond. For Bellamy, Taylor's remarks are nothing but cliched "common pulpit discourse." He thus only regrets "that instead of Taylor writing to Johnson, Johnson did not write to Taylor." If Taylor wants to do some good, he should publish "certain *Sermons*, said to be in his possession, and to be written by the literary Colossus, to whom this letter is addressed" (*General Magazine* 1 [June, 1787]: 18).

So warm a hope for excellent sermons was unusual. *The Monthly Mirror* later complained that many such collections suffer either from poor style, commonplace observations, or dull spirit. They "are soon laid aside: the reader does not find the edification he hoped to meet with."[5] That is not Johnson's case. In April 1788 Bellamy warmly reviews the sermon *For the Funeral of his Wife, Published by the Rev. Samuel Hayes*, and again asks that the other sermons be published. He has indeed "frequently heard Dr. Taylor in the pulpit; but, four-fifths of the discourses he delivered were certainly written by Dr. Johnson" (1 [April, 1788]: 199).

Bellamy gets his wish. In June 1788 he reviews the *Thirteen Sermons on different Subjects, Left for Publication by John Taylor, LL.D.* He both praises Johnson and scolds

4   Boswell so records on September 12, 1773 in Skye: "No wise man will be contented to die, if he thinks he is to fall into annihilation: for however unhappy any man's existence may be, he yet would rather have it, than not exist at all." Johnson also discussed annihilation when on September 16, 1777, he considered Hume's indifference to death. The topic reappears on April 15, 1788, when Johnson reasserts that "mere existence is so much better than nothing, that one would rather exist even in pain, than not exist." For these, see *Boswell's Life of Johnson, Together with Boswell's Journal of a Tour to the Hebrides and Johnson's Diary of a Journey into North Wales*, ed. George Birkbeck Hill, rev. L. F. Powell, 6 vols. (Oxford: Clarendon Press, 1934–1950), 5:180 (Skye, from the *Journey*), 3:153 (re: Hume), 3:295–296 (mere existence). Thomas Taylor reprints the *Letter* and briefly discusses contemporary response to it. See Taylor, *A Life of John Taylor LL. D. of Ashbourne* (London: St. Catherine Press and J. Nisbet, [1911]), 27–48.

5   *The Monthly Mirror* 18 (October 1804): 251. This reviews Samuel Clapham's collection of *Sermons, Selected and Abridged Chiefly from Minor Authors . . . For the Use of Families* (London: F. C. and J. Rivington et al., 1804). Clapham's collection is an exception to the general rule.

Taylor for appearing to take credit for Johnson's work. These are among the forty that Johnson himself said he had written:

> Why his name is not prefixed to them, we are at a loss to guess; and we are equally at a loss to guess why the Sermon on the death of his wife is not added to the number. These are not *all* the Sermons Taylor had of Johnson's composition: and it is greatly to be wished that the remainder of that great man's Discourses may be recovered from the different hands in which they are lodged. It ought, however, to be generally understood, that these *are* the Sermons of Johnson, for there are some who would read his Discourses, and might thereby reap great advantages, who cannot be tempted to peruse those of an ecclesiastic, especially an ecclesiastic of so little celebrity as Dr. Taylor, who ought himself to have been the Editor of these Discourses, or to have instructed Mr. H[ayes] to avow the author. (*General Magazine* 2 [June, 1788]: 311)

In August 1789 Bellamy celebrates the appearance of twelve more of Johnson's "discourses," together with the Tetty memorial sermon also "left for publication." Johnson's admirers may again "rejoice!" The admirable religious belief, style, and moral sentiments make plain that these are Mr. Rambler's invaluable issue. Bellamy goes beyond celebration. He again shows that he both knew Johnson and his work. As for the sermon on Tetty's death, we hear, he himself "well recollects, Dr. Taylor preaching or rather reading at Ashborne, in Derbyshire, before what is called a 'Benefit Society,' about the year 1777" (3 [August, 1789]: 354).

Bellamy's *General Magazine and Impartial Review* demonstrates that response to Johnson's religious tracts after his death was a lively topic of interest.[6] Bellamy and others resented Taylor's apparent pilfering of Johnson's proper intellectual canon. Scholarship on eighteenth-century religion, and on Johnson's role in that religion, have become important parts of historical reclamation, within which Bellamy's *General Magazine* plays its modest role.

3.

Given Bellamy's occasional presence in Johnson's company, he plays a useful part as well in correcting the notion that Johnson either was indifferent or hostile to the dramatic and to the painters' arts. Bellamy contributes to our ongoing skepticism that Boswell's

6   Bellamy was less keen on Johnson's *Prayers*, whose third edition he reviewed in 1796: They are the thoughts of a great man, but the prayers vary little, make the same pleas and repeated hopes for, this time, satisfaction of regularly offered resolutions. Nonetheless, "the private devotions of our great moralist evince all that fervour of genuine piety, which may be traced throughout his works." See *Monthly Mirror* 7 (June 1796): 98.

Johnson is the "real" Johnson. Here are episodes that Bellamy records in his memoir of the well-known later eighteenth-century portrait painter and actor William Parsons.

Parsons often was in David Garrick's company as he entered the final phases of his stage career. Garrick was aware that his powers were waning, and "has often said, 'PARSONS I will take my leave of the town, before its gradual absence whispers that falling off, of which I am but too conscious: this is one of JOHNSON's good natured hints, but I'll profit by it.'"[7] Parsons's Johnson does not regularly mock Garrick and actors in general. Instead, he emerges as an amiable guide aware of Garrick's vulnerabilities and of the audience's and fame's fickle nature. This Johnson understands the nature of audience as well as readers' responses. He understands the vanity of human wishes and how best to advise a proud, admired friend and companion who needs to cope with inevitable decline and often unkind nature's signal of retreat.

We see a non-Boswellian Johnson as well when he appears in another context to which he was supposedly hostile. Bellamy dabbled in poetry, music, and, at first reluctantly, visual arts. Parsons stiffens his spine, urges him to try portraiture, and encourages him as soon as he has paint and canvas at hand. After some feeble efforts, Bellamy improves enough to present an image to a group of exalted men of arts and letters, including Sir Joshua Reynolds, Johnson, and Goldsmith. Reynolds cannot take his eyes off the painting. Goldsmith says that it "was composed by a great man":

> "I do not know what you mean by composed," said Sir JOSHUA, "but it is the worst thing I ever saw in my life." "Why do you take so much notice of it then?" said GOLDSMITH. "Oh! Sir," said Dr. JOHNSON, "physicians always love to analyse the faces." "My reason," said Sir JOSHUA, "for noticing that picture is, that though taken altogether it is a very contemptible performance, yet the man who painted it has an uncommon correct eye for colouring." "There's a compliment for you, DIBDIN," said GOLDSMITH "why don't you make your best bow?" It finished by Sir JOSHUA's advising me to persevere, and promising to lend me some landscapes as models for my imitation.[8] (68)

This is not Boswell's bellicose, domineering master of London's written and spoken word. Johnson is characteristically perceptive, but he nonetheless is one speaker among several. He is deferential to Sir Joshua, the true leader of the group, whose knowledge of

---

7   Bellamy, *The Life of Mr. William Parsons, Comedian, Written by Thomas Bellamy* (London, 1795), 19. Subsequent citations are given in the text. Bellamy reissued the memoir in volume 2 of his *Miscellanies in Prose and Verse* (London, 1795). Both the *Life* and the *Miscellanies* were printed for the author rather than by an established bookseller under his own name.

8   See Bellamy's *Parsons*, 78. Goldsmith's mention of Charles Dibdin indicates that Bellamy's then-friend, the composer and musician Charles Dibdin, was part of the group. Villa-Real Gooch makes plain that Bellamy was a congenial companion: *Beggar Boy*, 1: xxxix, xliv–xlvi.

portraiture and ability to evaluate and encourage are at the heart of the episode. Nor is Goldsmith the amusing Boswellian dupe, but an approximately equal conversationalist who, like Johnson, wisely yields to the renowned specialist.

Bellamy's Garrick-episode shows us Johnson's wisdom recollected in anxiety and his good nature put to practical use. His Reynolds-episode shows us Johnson's role as part of a social group, rather than as the voice of the group. He was a member of the chorus rather than the solo basso profundo in each case. Thomas Bellamy enlarges our knowledge of Johnson. His image as the Great Cham of literature wants fleshing out with yet unreclaimed aspects of Johnsonian contexts. This is true as well for our understanding of Johnson's religion in general and of his sermons in particular. As Bellamy said in *The General Magazine and Impartial Review*, "every reader, who has either taste or virtue, will read them with avidity, and, we hope, with advantage" (3 [August, 1789]: 355). Bellamy's living and posthumous relationship with Johnson allows us to see him, or perhaps even glance at him, without the familiar characterizations by Boswell, Hawkins, and Piozzi.

That spirit of inquiry is shared by all the contributors to this volume, as it was shared by all the contributors to the Houghton's "Johnson at 300" symposium. Johnson after three hundred years is not the Johnson after two hundred years or any other celebratory number. Perhaps we are coming a bit closer to the benevolent complexity of Johnson's reputation, character, and achievement. To the question, then, What more is there to learn about Samuel Johnson? the answer must be a very great deal.

Johnson and Revolution

Nicholas Hudson

I N MAY 1687, KING JAMES II COMMANDED THE BISHOPS AND CLERGY of his kingdom to read aloud, for the second time, his Declaration of Indulgence on two consecutive Sundays. For many of the king's most ardent supporters, beleaguered by his repeated assaults on England's most revered institutions, this was the last straw. Contrary to his own promises, James had speedily prorogued a Tory parliament for failing to adhere strictly to his wishes. He had suspended Commissioners of the Peace, many belonging to England's oldest landed families, for not pledging to engineer a new Parliament packed with Catholics and loyal supporters. He had forced Catholic masters and presidents on colleges at Oxford University, the bastion of Toryism, even in defiance of their ancient statutes. Conversion to James's beloved Catholicism had become virtually a prerequisite for advancement in his government and even for high appointments in the army and civil service. Now he wished the clergy of the established church to proclaim aloud from their pulpits that, while he was sorry that they were not all Catholics, he had decreed an end to all prohibitions against any religious group to full participation in the state. Superficially, this sounded very liberal indeed. But even most Protestant dissenters suspected that they were being treacherously seduced to support James's efforts to enfold England in the arms of Rome and France. For staunch Anglicans, such as William Sancroft, the deeply Tory Archbishop of Canterbury, James had betrayed his vows to protect the established church and was plainly commanding them to act illegally. Sancroft and six other bishops approached the king at Westminster Palace on their knees, humbly beseeching him to relieve them of this duty.

Instead, the enraged king sent the bishops to the Tower to await trial for sedition. As the seven bishops sailed down the Thames from Westminster to the Tower, they were surrounded by boats full of well-wishers who asked their blessings. A delegation of Puritan divines visited the bishops in their confinement, thanking them for supporting the Protestant religion. The courtroom at their trial was filled with England's political and social elite, and when the king's packed jury pronounced the bishops not guilty, the cheer from the court emanated like waves over London. Everywhere bonfires were lit and effigies of the pope were set alight; bewigged Cavaliers embraced black-hatted Puritans in the street; everywhere, at least half-a-century of civil war and vicious sectarian strife dissolved in an epiphanic moment of national solidarity. James realized he had gone too far. For several months, he bargained for time, promising regular parliaments and the repeal of his most autocratic measures. Secretly, he planned his retreat, and as leading Tories and Whigs penned an invitation to his estranged daughter and son-in-law to invade England, he escaped in December 1688 towards France, throwing the Great Seal of office into the Thames. He was at first stopped at the coast, but escaped again, leaving London and his kingdom to William and Mary.[1]

For people of the eighteenth century, the events that I have described were known as the "Revolution," a term which stood less for a kind of political process than for this particular historical juncture. I will later return to Johnson's appropriate definition of "revolution" in the *Dictionary*, but here it is: "Change in the state of a government or country. It is used among us, κατ' εξοχήν, for the change produced by the admission of king William and queen Mary."[2] Johnson's use of the Greek term for "pre-eminently" (κατ' εξοχήν) indicates that, by 1755, he realized that the word "revolution" had already gained a wider currency in political discourse. It no longer meant just the accession of William and Mary, though the English label clearly influenced its later and broader use. In 1779, the United States Continental Congress issued a defense of what it called the "American Revolution," asserting that the former colonies had affirmed the principles of the Revolution of 1688 and implying that Britain had betrayed its own revolutionary values.[3] In 1792, Condorcet declared that what he called the "French Revolution" was "exactly similar to that of the English," except that the French had finished the job that the English had failed to complete.[4] By the late eighteenth century, in other words, the word "revolution" had ramified and abstracted itself in ways that, ironically, made the Revolution of 1688 seem like not much of a "revolution" at all. Inspired by successive American, French, Russian, and Chinese revolutions, and having wandered through many a *Plaza de la Revolution*, political scientists have since developed a literature devoted to defining, in abstract terms, what actually counts as a "revolution."[5] For

1   My account relies a great deal on Tim Harris, *Revolution: The Great Crisis of the British Monarchy, 1685–1720* (London: Penguin, 2007). It does not seem, however, that modern historians differ in factual details in significant ways from Thomas Babington Macaulay's *History of England from the Accession of James II*, which I use here from the Everyman edition (London: J.M. Dent; New York: E.P. Dutton 1906), even if historians disagree about his political interpretation of these events.

2   Samuel Johnson, *A Dictionary of the English Language on CD-ROM*, ed. Anne McDermott (Cambridge: Cambridge University Press, 1996).

3   United States Continental Congress, *Observations on the American Revolution* (Philadelphia, 1779). See especially the letter written by the Congress to George III, and reprinted, 13.

4   Jean-Antoine-Nicolas de Caritat, Marquis de Condorcet, *Reflections on the English Revolution of 1688, and that of the French* (London: Printed for James Ridgway, 1792), 1, and throughout.

5   Helpful as general surveys of debates in political history and political science are Charles Tilly, *European Revolutions 1492–1992* (Oxford: Blackwell, 1993); and Stephen K. Sanderson, *Revolutions: A Worldwide Introduction to Political and Social Change* (Boulder, Colo.: Paradigm, 2005). For scholars of the British eighteenth century, the interest of these studies lies in their fundamental disinterest in eighteenth-century Britain, an age preoccupied with ideas of "revolution."

reasons that I will explain, the Revolution of 1688 seldom makes the cut.[6] Though the English arguably invented the term in its nascent political sense, it is a very fusty English person indeed who would expound today, over his or her pint, about the glories of 1688. The historical denigration of the Revolution of 1688 crosses many political lines. For Marxist historians in the tradition of Christopher Hill, the real "English Revolution" occurred not in 1688 but in 1642, when the rising bourgeoisie appropriately rose up to decapitate the monarchy and abolish the House of Lords.[7] For these historians, the Revolution of 1688 was an afterpiece, a dramatic confirmation of a structural change that had already occurred. At the other end of the political spectrum, J.C.D. Clark has denied that any revolutions occurred between 1642 and 1832 because England remained fundamentally an ancien régime.[8] William III and subsequent monarchs, he claims, might be deemed even more powerful politically than Charles I, who discovered that his power was actually very little. Interestingly, even one important tradition of Whig interpretations of the Revolution of 1688 concedes, similarly, that this event was not essentially revolutionary, for it only reaffirmed the ancient rights and constitution of England in the face of James's tyrannical innovations. This position, very common in Johnson's day, found its way into Thomas Babington Macaulay's *History of England* (1848–1859) which, despite its title, is mostly a history of the Revolution of 1688 and the reign of William III. For Macaulay, William was a great hero because he restored and protected, rather than changed, the English constitution undermined by Charles II and his brother James. Flighty Frenchmen might have real revolutions, but Britons (and maybe heroic Dutchmen) instead bullishly resist assaults on freedoms written in the blood-line of the Anglo-Saxon race.

These debates about what counts as a genuine "revolution," and whether Britain ever had one, are not the subject of the following essay. Our abstractions and definitions indeed beg the question of why, whatever we think, English, Welsh, Scots, and Irish people of the eighteenth century generally believed that something transformative had occurred when William marched peaceably into London in December 1688. In the words of such an astute observer as David Hume in his *History of England* (1754–1762),

---

6   The status of the Revolution of 1688 as a genuine revolution has recently been defended by Steven Pincus in *1688: The First Modern Revolution* (New Haven: Yale University Press, 2009).

7   See Christopher Hill, *The Century of Revolution, 1603–1714*, 2nd ed. (London and New York: W.W. Norton, 1980). The legacy of Hill's attitudes is obvious in Terry Eagleton, *Rape of Clarissa* (Oxford: Blackwell, 1982), 1, where 1688 confirms a total dominance of the "bourgeoisie."

8   See J.C.D. Clark, *English Society, 1688–1832: Ideology, Social Structure, and Political Practice during the Ancien Regime* (Cambridge: Cambridge University Press, 1985); and *Revolution and Rebellion: State and Society in England in the Seventeenth and Eighteenth Centuries* (Cambridge: Cambridge University Press, 1986).

"The revolution forms a new epoch in the constitution."[9] Even those, including Hume, who believed that the Revolution confirmed or clarified an ancient division of powers declared that the nation had leapt to a new plateau by this very act of elucidation. They also recognized that the Revolution could be interpreted in many different ways, and that debates about the nature and significance of the Revolution did not belong merely to dusty archives explored by historians like us. For them, the historical text of 1688 was fertile with innumerable political possibilities, a fertility that Burke confronted in his *Reflections on the Revolution in France* (1790), a book about how, essentially, the Revolution of 1688 had been dangerously misinterpreted. Interpretations of the Revolution indeed acted as a barometer of political allegiance, segregating not only Whig from Tory, but increasingly Whig from Whig, Burke's "Old Whigs" from the radical members of Revolution Societies.

Positioning Samuel Johnson within this gamut of opinion thus elucidates his ideological relationship to the past, present and future of Britain. Johnson actually had a great deal to say about the Revolution of 1688, and his views, while not always free from evasion and misconstruction, represent a singular and thoughtful reaction to this great event, contributing to our abiding historical dialogue about the nature of revolution itself. In recent scholarship, Johnson's understanding of the Revolution has generally been subordinated to an affiliated yet separate issue, his attitudes to Jacobitism and the exiled Stuart family. This is a *distinct* issue because one could support the need to replace James II while continuing to deny the strict legitimacy of William III, an admittedly awkward and even illogical position adopted by five of the seven famous bishops, and most non-jurors. Moreover, one could admit the necessity of the Revolution, yet continue to regret that it had occurred. This regret stemmed not from an adherence to the early Stuart doctrine of the divine right of kings, but from an anxiety that replacing even an intolerable king had severely undermined popular respect for government, shaking the very foundations of the social order. This position, as I will argue, seems very close to Johnson's, at least in his mature years. There is virtually no evidence that Johnson ever seriously believed in the divine right of the Stuarts. My reader might recall Johnson's jokey defense of divine right when, having said to a pretty young woman "My dear, I hope you are Jacobite,"[10] he was obliged to explain himself to her annoyed father. Yet, in the Vinerian law lectures that he co-wrote with Sir Robert Chambers, *jure divino* is identified with an "age of prejudice and

9   David Hume, *The History of England from the Invasion of Julius Caesar to the Revolution of 1688*, 6 vols. (Indianapolis, Ind.: Liberty Classics, 1983–1985), 6:531.

10   *Boswell's Life of Samuel Johnson, Together with Boswell's Journal of a Tour to the Hebrides and Johnson's Diary of a Journey into North Wales*, ed. George Birkbeck Hill, rev. L.F. Powell, 6 vols. (Oxford: Clarendon Press, 1934–1950), 1:430 (hereafter cited as *Boswell's Life*).

ignorance" when law-makers found it necessary to "invest the king with something of a sacred character" in order to secure obedience.[11]

I should clarify that Johnson's denial of the divine right of kings does not imply that he was therefore a Whig or a "liberal." Johnson's commitment to the need to maintain reverence for kingship represents a central tenet of his political attitudes, especially after 1760—that capital date—when Johnson moved from an Opposition stance to the position of George III's supporter. In the following essay, I will present evidence towards the argument, professedly controversial, that the young Johnson was, in fact, closer to Whiggism than the older "Tory" known to Boswell. That is, he moved not away, but *towards*, views that might be misconstrued as Jacobite. For this reason, it is not surprising that Jacobite readings of Johnson tend to rummage through statements Johnson made in Boswell's hearing during the last two years of his life when, sick and disillusioned, he reflected on the damage done to monarchial authority by the Revolution. Viewed against this amorphous political background, Johnson's political attitudes seem far from static, and his growing distrust of certain radical Whig interpretations of the Revolution far from atavistic. Indeed, they seem in many respects highly prescient, for one can almost imagine the ghost of Johnson whispering to his old friend Burke in 1790: "I told you so." Near the end of the following essay, I will again try to summon the ghost of Johnson to tell us about the French Revolution.

I have emphasized a moving political backdrop: in connection with the Revolution, Johnson reacted to a climate of opinion that progressed through a number of successive phases. The first of these phases marked the very minting of the word "revolution" in a political sense, leading, gradually, to the proud declaration of this term by Americans in 1776 and by the French in 1789. It has been often noted that "revolution" originally referred to the movement of the earth around the sun, and that this astronomical term therefore denoted not transformation, but rather a return to the beginning, the *status quo ante*.[12] This etymology is not strictly accurate. My scan through some two thousand titles containing the word "revolution" between 1640 and 1790 suggests, indeed, that very few applied this term to political events before 1688, after which there occurred an explosion of extensions of this originally astronomical term not only to political events in Britain but to upheavals in the ancient and modern worlds. Before 1688, the most

11   Sir Robert Chambers and Samuel Johnson, *A Course of Lectures on the English Law: Delivered at the University of Oxford, 1767–1773*, ed. Thomas M. Curley, 2 vols. (Madison: University of Wisconsin Press, 1986), 1:154.

12   See Vernon F. Snow, "The Concept of Revolution in Seventeenth-Century England," *Historical Journal* 5 (1962): 167–174; J.R. Western, *Monarchy and Revolution; the English State in the 1680's* (Totowa, N.J.: Rowman and Littlefield, 1972), 1; Harris, *Revolution*, 34.

common appearance of the word "revolution" was in the title of an almanac published from 1654 until the 1730s, Richard Saunders's *Apollo Anglicanus: The English Apollo; Assisting all Persons in the Right Understanding of this Years Revolution*. As one would expect from an almanac, this annual publication did not interpret the revolution of the sun as merely a return to the beginning, but as the inauguration of a new phase, of a different orientation of universal forces. Every year delivered a new schedule of tides and weather, a new prognosis of days of sickness and health, of opportunity or danger, all meticulously charted by Saunders (who actually died in 1675) and by his surviving cohorts. Even in its etymological roots, then, "revolution" meant not the same thing all over again, but a whole new phase of the sun.

"Revolution" implied something more: it suggested that forces beyond human ken, the rotation of planets, perhaps the mysterious operations of God Himself, controlled human events. Here let us think back to the narrative of the Revolution that opened this essay. Immediate reactions to the occurrences of 1687 to 1689 emphasize an unexpected, even miraculous, confluence of events. No one had expected James II merely to run away; no one had thought that a Calvinist Dutchman, invited by both Whigs and Tories, would arrive virtually unopposed to a metropolis filled with citizens, waving oranges at the end of sticks. The very day of William's landing at Torbay, November 5, seemed strangely providential, for this was the anniversary of the Gunpowder Plot, and one day after William's birthday. The very winds had changed course to secure the Prince of Orange's safe arrival. The belief that the Revolution signaled an act of God, a "deliverance" allowed through a strange reconfiguration of forces, played handily into Whig justifications of this dynastic change. This Whig interpretation would be summarized in 1725 by Laurence Echard, the first author to write a history of England under his name alone: "If *England* had been govern'd at that Time by any other *Popish* Prince and Ministry, it wou'd have met with no *Deliverance* at all; and if that Deliverance had been wrought by any other Person, than he that did effect it, the Benefit had never been of any settled or lasting Duration."[13]

Echard is a fine and neglected historian in ways that this citation might not immediately suggest: he understood the Revolution and all great events in English history as moments when long-standing pressures in the state found vent at an instant when personalities and historical contingencies arrived at an apt and critical conjuncture. Echard, an Anglican priest, predictably attributed these moments not to Fortune, but to acts of God. His interpretation of the Revolution nevertheless strikes me as defensible in modern, secular terms. The Revolution might never have occurred; it did occur, to crystallize Echard's implication, because James was very foolish, and William was not. Yet the notion that the Revolution had ignited for reasons beyond human agency could also have a strong Tory and even Jacobite application. A doctrine

13   Laurence Echard, *The History of the Revolution, and the Establishment of England in the Year 1688* (London: Printed for Jacob Tonson, 1725), 271.

preached at many an Anglican pulpit of the seventeenth-century, as by Bishop Sancroft, was the duty of passive obedience and non-resistance to the king. If events forced even Sancroft to ride passively down the Thames to the Tower, then he was not really "resisting," and the Revolution implied nothing at all about the rights of the "people" to resist a monarch who had breached the supposed contract to serve and protect them.

The attempt to square the Revolution with the doctrine of non-resistance, and, indeed, with yearnings for a Jacobite restoration, came to a head when Henry Sacheverell delivered his inflammatory sermon *The Perils of False Brethren* at St. Paul's on November 5, 1709. Whig and lower-Church outrage against this sermon focused less on Sacheverell's hatred of dissenters, the "false brethren" whom he portrayed as inherently seditious, than on his alleged suggestion that the Revolution involved no resistance at all. As the Whig Lord Lechmere argued at Sacheverell's impeachment, the people had, of course, "resisted" the king at the Revolution, "Thereby plainly founding that Power, and Right of Resistance which was exercised by the People at the time of the happy Revolution, and which the Duties of Self-Preservation and Religion call'd upon them to, upon the Necessity of the Case."[14] Sacheverell responded that if the Revolution resulted from "necessity," then it implied no actual "resistance."[15] He had by no means impugned the Revolution, as charged, but merely insisted that it was a "necessary" event that did not establish resistance to a bad monarch as a constitutional principle. Looking back to the letter of his sermon, Sacheverell had indeed preached exactly this, even attributing the doctrine of non-resistance to William himself. In his declaration upon landing at Torbay, the Prince of Orange had after all denied that he was resisting James, and meant only to permit the English Parliament to make what decisions it wished.[16]

Here we have entered into the terrain of heavy metaphysics, if not equivocation. Does complying with "necessity," or an act of God, imply agency or establish any principles for future action? Johnson, in any event, hated metaphysics. Although the idea of "necessity" informs virtually every statement that he made about the Revolution, as we will see, he would not tolerate any cant denying that the English people actively resisted the measures of James II. As he wrote in his "Introduction to the Political State of Great Britain" (1756), published in *The Literary Magazine* when Johnson remained fully in opposition to the Newcastle administration, "the necessity of self-preservation . . . impelled the subjects of James to drive him from the throne." Of particular importance here are the active verbs: "believing that there was no religion without popery," he explained, James "impelled" the people to "drive" him from the

14   *The Tryal of Dr. Henry Sacheverell* (London: Printed for Jacob Tonson, 1710), 34.

15   Ibid., 11–12.

16   See Henry Sacherverell, *The Perils of False Brethren both in Church and State* (London: Printed for Henry Clements, 1709), 11–12.

throne.[17] James was "driven from his palace," he wrote in *The False Alarm* (1770).[18] In other words, Johnson had no truck with Sacheverell's attempts to portray the Revolution as an event lacking in human agency; he remained far closer to the position upheld by Sacheverell's impeachers, who insisted that the Revolution was indeed an act of defiance.

Moreover, Johnson found no trouble in attributing this agency to the people, the "subjects of James." Boswell recorded this disquisition in 1775: "*We*, who thought that we should *not* be saved if we were Roman Catholics, had the merit of maintaining our religion, at the expense of submitting ourselves to the government of King William, (for it could not be done otherwise)."[19] Plainly, necessity, in Johnson's opinion, did not entail lack of resistance. His trenchant realism on this issue helps to explain his statement that "I never . . . knew a non-juror who could reason," much praised in Lord Macaulay's *History*.[20] How could a logical person both help to overthrow a king and yet remain loyal to that king, the case of most original non-jurors? At a later stage, particularly at the Hanoverian Succession, how could one abjure a reigning monarch whose authority made one's personal livelihood or prosperity achievable? Johnson's criticisms of non-jurors stress the danger of exposing oneself to poverty and consequent criminality on a principle that, as he implies, hardly ranks as a matter of life and death.[21]

Nevertheless, Johnson also shared the early Tory hostility toward those who wished to extend the story of the Revolution into a justification of contractual kingship and the principle of resistance itself. He was indeed inclined to avoid language that glorified the Revolution of 1688. Here we might return to his definition of "revolution" in his *Dictionary*: "Change in the state of a government or country. It is used among us, κατ' εξοχήν, for the change produced by the admission of king William and queen Mary." This definition hardly sparkles with patriotic zeal, as remarked by his critics. "What noble words!" jeered Wilkes in *The North Briton*, "what a bold, glowing expression!"[22] Johnson did indeed appear to spice up the definition in his 1773 revision of the *Dictionary*

17   Samuel Johnson, "An Introduction to the Political State of Great Britain," in *Political Writings*, in *The Yale Edition of the Works of Samuel Johnson*, ed. Donald J. Greene, vol. 10 (New Haven and London: Yale University Press, 1977), 142 (hereafter cited as *Political Writings*).

18   *Political Writings*, 342.

19   *Boswell's Life*, 2:341.

20   *Boswell's Life*, 4:286. See Thomas Babington Macaulay, *History of England from the Accession of James II*, 4 vols. (London: J.M. Dent & Sons; New York: E.P. Dutton and Co., 1906), 3:59 and Macaulay's note. Macaulay adds that Johnson made the rather perplexing exception of Charles Leslie, who played virtually no part in the Revolution of 1688.

21   See *Boswell's Life*, 2:321–322, and Johnson's reflection on Elijah Fenton's "perverseness of integrity" for refusing to take the oaths at Cambridge, "Life of Fenton," in *The Lives of the Poets*, ed. Roger Lonsdale, 4 vols. (Oxford: Clarendon Press, 2006), 3:89.

22   *The North Briton*, no. 12 (August 21, 1762).

by adding an illustration from, of all places, Charles Davenant's economic treatise, *A Discourse upon Grants and Resumptions*: "The late *revolution*, justified by its necessity, and the good it has produced, will be a lasting answer." This sounds more enthusiastic, and even hints that the Revolution did serve as a constitutional precedent. Johnson must have known, however, that Davenant had been a strong supporter of James, and that, though finally reconciled to the Revolution Settlement, long endured the official stigma of Jacobitism. Moreover, Johnson had edited Davenant's original passage. Here is what Davenant wrote: "The late revolution, justified by its necessity, and the good it has produced, will be a lasting answer *to all that foolish doctrine* [emphasis added]." The "foolish doctrine" that Davenant meant was the "wrong principles of unlimited obedience due to the unlimited exercise of power"—that is, the doctrine of passive obedience.[23] There are many reasons why Johnson may have made this change. Perhaps he wished merely to be concise. It does seem significant, however, that he chose to remain silent and ambiguous on what exact "answer" the Revolution had provided.

A similar kind of grudging ambiguity often characterized Johnson's depiction of the principal actors in the Revolution. At times, he expressed considerable disdain for James II's failures as a king. In *The False Alarm*, he referred to "the dangerous bigotry of James."[24] In "Life of Waller," he describes James as having embarked on a "holy war" against the English church, and obviously approves of Waller's spirited defense of Anglicanism to the monarch's face.[25] Clearly, Johnson did not believe a word of James's proclaimed tolerance for all religions, as pretended in the Declaration of Indulgence. In "Life of Sprat," he broached another notorious innovation of James's reign, his creation of an Ecclesiastical Commission to prosecute those who defied the royal will in religious matters. For reasons of "interest or obedience," as Johnson observes, the Anglican Bishop Sprat sat on this commission along side others such as Judge Jeffries, the villain of the Bloody Assizes. Sprat, though, refused to participate in the commission's campaign against those who refused to read the Declaration of Indulgence, which Sprat himself had recited only with extreme reluctance, his hands shaking on the pulpit, according to Macaulay's colorful description.[26] "Further he refused to go . . . ," wrote Johnson, "he wrote to the lords and other commissioners a formal profession of his unwillingness to exercise that authority any longer." This, as Johnson went on, spelled the end of James's hated commission.[27] *Pace* J.C.D. Clark,

23   Charles Davenant, *The Political and Commercial Works of that Celebrated Writer Charles D'Avenant*, ed. Sir Charles Whitworth, 5 vols. (London: Printed for Jacob Tonson, 1771), 3:16.

24   *Political Writings*, 342.

25   *Lives of the Poets*, 2:42.

26   Macaulay, *History of England*, 2:145.

27   *Lives of the Poets*, 2:186.

such descriptions of the Revolution hardly seem like "studied neutrality."[28] Indeed, Johnson's remarks on the events of James's reign occasionally approach satire. In "Life of Dryden," he remarked as follows on this poet's celebration of the birth of the Prince of Wales, the future Old Pretender, very near the end of James's reign: "Now was the time for Dryden to rouse his imagination, and strain his voice. Happy days were at hand, and he was willing to enjoy and diffuse the anticipated blessings." This is followed by perhaps Johnson's most withering statement on the vanity of Jacobite wishes. "A few months passed after these joyful notes, and every blossom of popish hope was blasted for ever by the Revolution."[29]

This sounds very decisive. On the other hand, it would be inaccurate to construe Johnson's most damning remarks on James as a *celebration* of the Revolution or an endorsement of what his Whig contemporaries called "Revolution Principles." Johnson could also express considerable sympathy for those who remained loyal to James, even after all he had done. He applauds Sprat for "manfully" standing up for his deposed master after the Revolution.[30] Johnson could even sound curiously sympathetic to James II. James "was not ignorant of the real interest of his country," he wrote in "An Introduction to the Political State of Great Britain," for "he desired its power and its happiness, and thought rightly, that there was no happiness without religion." James's only great mistake, Johnson suggested, was in "very erroneously and absurdly" thinking that "there was no religion without popery."[31] Indeed, it is Johnson's loyalty to the established church that dominates his statements about the "necessity" of the Revolution. At no point does he mention other serious allegations against James II— that this king used his supposed "dispensing" power to override the laws of England, that he connived and cheated to fill great offices with incompetent sycophants, that he increasingly collaborated with the imperial designs of Louis XIV. Johnson had virtually nothing good to say about the Whig heroes of the Revolution. He apparently admitted to Rev. Robert Maxwell that these Whigs, unlike modern Whigs, were not without principles.[32] On the subject of the great Dutch deliverer, Johnson showed very little propensity to be grateful. He reflected repeatedly on William's "gloomy sullenness," his "brutality," his narrow preoccupation with war and the interests of his native Holland.[33]

---

28   J.C.D. Clark, *Samuel Johnson: Literature and English Cultural Politics from the Restoration to Romanticism* (Cambridge: Cambridge University Press, 1994), 234.

29   *Lives of the Poets*, 2:105–106.

30   *Lives of the Poets*, 2:186.

31   *Political Writings*, 142.

32   See *Boswell's Life*, 2:117.

33   See *Political Writings*, 342; review of *The Account of the Conduct of the Dowager Dutchess of Marlborough* (*Gentleman's Magazine*, May 1742), in *The Works of Samuel Johnson, LL.D.*, 11 vols. (Oxford: Talboys and Wheeler; London: W. Pickering, 1825), 6:6–7; "Life of Addison," in *Lives of the Poets*, 3:3.

How can we harmonize Johnson's varying and apparently inconsistent statements about the Revolution? These statements, deployed selectively, have justified readings of him as both a Jacobite and as a constitutional Whig. On the one hand, he acknowledged the necessity of James's overthrow and refused to echo early Tory cant about passive obedience. On the other hand, he refused to corroborate "Revolution Principles," the supposed right of Englishmen to overthrow an unjust king or to join very fully in the demonization of James as an infatuated tyrant. To decipher this complicated record, we need to return again to the unfolding story of how the Revolution was being re-interpreted after the trial of Sacheverell and the Hanoverian Succession.

In *A Dissertation upon Parties* (1735), Lord Bolingbroke declared that the debate about passive obedience and non-resistance was defunct and that any meaningful distinction between Whigs and Tories had been dissolved. Bolingbroke was a brilliant but highly devious politician who served as the Pretender's secretary of state before recanting and returning to England. We should take anything he writes with a large grain of salt. Nevertheless, what he claimed in this treatise and elsewhere strongly prefigured the tone of political debate from his own time into the reign of George III. The Revolution had been a formative event, he wrote, but its original ends had been lost, and its successes reversed. Hanoverian monarchs could no longer wave around prerogative or dispensing powers in the style of the early Stuarts and, most egregiously, James II. Through the power of *"Corruption,"* the nefarious influence of placemen and sleazy backroom deals, parliament had become a chessboard of monarchial influence, making the king and his favorites as powerful as ever. Corruption had become prerogative in another guise.[34] For Bolingbroke, that guise took the form of the ample and gaudily dressed Sir Robert Walpole, his pockets bulging with bribes and sinecures. Philosophical leader of the "Patriot Opposition" that formed against Walpole in the 1730s, Bolingbroke forged a connection between courtly corruption and kingly prerogative—a supposed reprisal of James II's dispensary power—that became a major theme in political discourse of this period. Caught up in this discontent was the young Johnson, newly arrived in London. In *London* (1738), a Juvenalian expression of conventional Opposition charges, he lamented corruption and the renewed power of the court. In *Marmor Norfolciense* (1739), he notoriously implied that the emblematic white "horse" of Hanover was draining the veins of the leonine English nation. This vision led to an ominous warning: "Kings change their laws, and kingdoms change their kings."[35]

34   Henry St. John, Lord Bolingbroke, *A Dissertation upon Parties* (Dublin: Re-printed for G. Faulkner et al., 1735), 181, and throughout.

35   *Political Writings*, 25, 37.

Should we fall into the revisionist habit of decoding this imagery into a barely cryptic Jacobitism?[36] In fact, Johnson's implication could be taken as virtually the *opposite* from Jacobite politics: in this interpretation, he threatens George and his Prime Minister with a new "Glorious Revolution," a reassertion of the power of the people against prerogative in a new form. Here I reintroduce my earlier thesis that Johnson became progressively less, rather than more, attached to Whig ideology, for *Marmor Norfolciense* is arguably the most pro-Revolution of 1688 piece that Johnson ever wrote. The pro-Revolution disposition of *Marmor* is substantiated by a detail late in this satire. Johnson's absurd narrator, the sycophantic translator of the slate disinterred from Walpole's Norfolk turf, finally proposes that the government establish a "*Society of Commentators*" composed of loyal men who avoid writings about "liberty and independency." This society, at the paltry charge of "65000ol.," could be set up at the Greenwich Hospital for naval veterans.[37] This was the hospital established by none other than William III in honor of his recently deceased wife, Mary II, who had made this hospital her pet project.[38] Hence, for all the evasive ironies of *Marmor*, the following message seems quite clear. George II and his favorite Walpole were reversing the gains of the Revolution, crushing "liberty and independency" through the insidious power of venality rather than open contempt for the laws. A symbol of the Revolution, Christopher Wren's Greenwich Hospital, might as well be desecrated.

Equally, however, I would resist Donald J. Greene's inference that Johnson continued to endorse some version of "Revolution Principles" throughout his life.[39] For all his early participation in Opposition politics, the older Johnson increasingly recoiled from knee-jerk Opposition even to good kings, and from the hysterical inference that all kings sought to subvert British liberties through corruption. With the final evaporation of Robinocracy, and particularly after the accession of George III, he scorned jeremiads such as the following: "The power of the Crown, almost dead and rotten as Prerogative, has grown up anew, with much more strength, and far less odium, under the name of Influence."[40] These are the words of Edmund Burke in his 1770 *Thoughts on the Cause of the Present Discontents*. In this widely admired tract, Burke painted a dark canvass of courtly intrigue worthy of hostile histories of Charles

36   See, for example, Howard Erskine-Hill, "Johnson the Jacobite?: A Response to the New Introduction to Donald Greene's *The Politics of Samuel Johnson*," *The Age of Johnson* 7 (1996): 11–12.

37   *Political Writings*, 45–50.

38   Macaulay, *History of England*, 4:119

39   See Donald J. Greene, *The Politics of Samuel Johnson* (New Haven: Yale University Press, 1960). In this famous book, Greene wrote little about the Revolution of 1688, but contended that Johnson was a liberal suspicious of monarchy and strongly inclined to individualism and popular rights.

40   Edmund Burke, *Thoughts on the Cause of the Present Discontents*, ed. Paul Langford, in *The Writings and Speeches of Edmund Burke*, gen. ed. Paul Langford, 9 vols. (Oxford : Clarendon Press, 1980–   ), 2:258.

II's "Cabal" or James II's inner-circle of Jesuits. Around George III had assembled a shadowy association called "the King's Friends" who in every nook and cranny of Westminster passed promissory notes and muttered winking assurances of the king's high regard. How bad had the corrupt authority of the crown become? "There is, in my opinion," Burke wrote, "a peculiar venom and malignity in this political distemper beyond that I have heard and read of."[41]

To imply that the court of George III sinned beyond the crimes of James II seems shocking indeed, though we should be careful of reading Burke too literally. The golden age of political rhetoric during the reign of George III was also a bronze age of hot air. For all Burke's brilliance, he blew as hot as anyone else. In historical retrospect, the history of George III's early reign seems rather the tragicomedy of an idealistic, but naive, young monarch trained by his tutor Lord Bute to believe in Bolingbroke's ideals of "the Patriot King," a virtuous father to his people who transcended the meaningless contentions of party. The young George embraced this ideal, honored Tories like Johnson, and dutifully toured farms and manufactures, only to be ridiculed as "Farmer George." For twenty-four years he tried vainly to find a balance between his own authority and the need to respect parliament, bargaining with a bewildering series of Old Guard worthies who in turn lectured him on his duties and left when he became obstinate. If this was an ancien régime, it was a regime haunted by his grandfather George II's exasperated cry: "The Ministers are the Kings in this country."[42] The Patriot King was an idea better in theory than in practice. For all George III's efforts to embody this ideal, he was instead branded with the alleged absolutism of the early Stuarts. These insinuations reached a climax in April 1780 when John Dunning made his motion that the "influence of the crown has increased, is increasing, and ought to be diminished," easily passed in the House of Commons. Charles James Fox, who called George III "Satan" in his correspondence, called this victory "a second revolution."[43]

Influenced by a Namierite tradition of eighteenth-century scholarship, we might be surprised to hear such rebellious language at a time when, allegedly, Whig oligarchs rotated calmly through the king's levee. Yet Burke, that later doughty conservative, was writing in 1770 that "there is something particularly alarming at the present conjuncture. There is hardly a man in or out of power who holds any other language."[44] In response to Dunning's motion, Lord North accused the opposition of "pursuing measures likely to overturn the constitution." In the House of Lords, the Duke of Manchester publicly referred to the execution of Charles I and the expulsion of James

---

41   Burke, *Writings and Speeches*, 2:282–283.

42   Cited in Paul Langford, *A Polite and Commercial People: England 1727–1783* (Oxford: Clarendon Press, 1989), 195.

43   See L.G. Mitchell, *Charles James Fox* (Oxford: Oxford University Press, 1992), 51; Langford, *Polite and Commercial People*, 548.

44   Burke, *Thoughts on the Cause of the Present Discontents*, 2:253.

II "for offences against the constitution, of infinitely less magnitude than those which marked the administration of the present reign."[45] Rumblings in radical circles were, predictably, even more venomous and threatening. Catherine Macaulay, in her *History of England, from the Revolution to the Present Time* (1763–83), sharpened a new arrow in the radical arsenal: the Revolution of 1688, she wrote, was a failure, a ruse, a coup d'état engineered by an aristocratic faction to install a new tyrant, and thus needed to be overthrown by a true republican revolution.[46]

To what degree did Johnson share the anxiety that dark clouds of social upheaval were gathering over Britain during the early reign of George III? In contrast to his early Opposition writing, he certainly did not believe that the king's influence had grown too powerful; indeed, as he told Adam Fergusson, "The crown has not power enough."[47] Nor did he express much concern for the supposed corruption of politics, and the backroom influence of the "King's Friends." The king had every right, he insisted, to use what means were at hand to spread royal influence.[48] The title of his pamphlet on Wilkesite agitation surrounding the Middlesex Election, *The False Alarm*, indicates his desire to pacify rhetorical clamors of rebellion and to put present discontents in their proper perspective. "We hear nothing," he wrote, virtually quoting Burke's *Thoughts on the Cause of the Present Discontents*, "but an alarming crisis of violated rights, and expiring liberties."[49] He expressed disgust at "low-born railers" who so abused "the only king" since Charles II who "much appeared to desire, or much endeavoured to deserve" the "affections of the people."[50] This revealing statement corresponds with many others he made about monarchs past and present.

In 1742, in a review of the Duchess of Marlborough's memoirs, he directly contrasted the genial populism of Charles II with the sullen insularity of William III: "Charles the second, by his affability and politeness, made himself the idol of the nation which he betrayed and sold. William the third was, for his insolence and brutality, hated by that people, which he protected and enriched."[51] This statement, though written at a time when some have thought Johnson a thorough-going Jacobite, contains the most open admission of William's virtues that he ever made. William had "protected and enriched" the nation. His 1742 statement also acknowledged what Johnson tended, later, to gloss over in his statements about Charles II: that king had "betrayed" the nation by

---

45   Langford, *Polite and Commercial People*, 547.

46   See Catherine Macaulay, *The History of England from the Revolution to the Present Time* (Bath, 1778), 4–5. See also Macaulay's reply to Burke's *Observations on a Pamphlet, entitled, Thoughts on the Cause of the Present Discontents* (London: Dilly, 1770).

47   *Boswell's Life*, 2:170.

48   See *Boswell's Life*, 2:355.

49   *Political Writings*, 335.

50   *Political Writings*, 342.

51   *Works* (1825), 6:7.

entering into private negotiations with Louis XIV to promote Catholicism in exchange for French subsidies. Johnson's judgments here seem almost startling; he subordinated the real accomplishments of these kings to superficial qualities of popular charm. Yet again and again it was William's rudeness and lack of public appeal which provoked Johnson's particular ire, not the supposed illegitimacy of his accession. With respect to George III, Johnson seems genuinely to have admired this Hanoverian's efforts to reach out to the people and to be, as he wrote in *The False Alarm*, "common father of all his people."[52] George was "the finest gentleman I have ever seen," he enthused after an audience in the king's library. "His manners," he went on, "are those of as fine a gentleman as we may suppose Lewis the Fourteenth or Charles the Second."[53]

Such sentiments might appear unworthy of a grave philosopher hostile to superficial thinking and emotive cant. Yet Johnson's belief that a monarch should be valued and even reverenced by the people explains a great deal about his abhorrence of public abuse of George III during the 1770s and 1780s. He increasingly came to think, moreover, that this abuse was doing real damage and foreshadowed, as Burke and others prognosticated, an approaching crisis. Despite his scorn for false alarms in 1770, Johnson's views over the next fourteen years grew increasingly gloomy and apprehensive. "I have lived to see things all as bad they can be," he said in 1783. "This reign has been very unfortunate." And in response to Pitt's Reform Bill the same year, "I am afraid of a civil war."[54] Many factors may have contributed to Johnson's late gloom. We sometimes underrate the swoon of national confidence caused by the final loss of America, an event widely ascribed to the incompetence of the king, or at least of his Prime Minister Lord North, whom Johnson came to despise. These late jeremiads also continued his long-term conviction that "Subordination is sadly broken down in this age." There is, he added, "a general relaxation of reverence."[55] For all Johnson's support for George III, the royal magic had not worked, and his diagnosis of this failure drew on the legacy of the Revolution. "Sir," he said to General Oglethorpe in 1783, "the want of inherent right in the King occasions all this disturbance. What we did at the Revolution was necessary: but it broke our constitution."[56] Earlier the same year, Boswell records that "He talked with regret and indignation of the factious opposition to Government at this time, and imputed it in a great measure to the Revolution."[57]

Let us add up these various statements. Johnson admired George III, welcoming his populism and what he, at least, perceived as the king's regal demeanor. He never ceased to think that "we," the English people, had performed a "necessary" act in

---

52 *Political Writings*, 344.

53 *Boswell's Life*, 2:41.

54 Ibid., 4:173, 200, 165.

55 Ibid., 3:262.

56 Ibid., 4:170–171.

57 Ibid., 4:164–165.

overthrowing James II. Against the line taken by some scholars, these statements do not imply an abiding Jacobitism. My thesis is that these statements do intimate a philosophy of kingship and civil order. Johnson evidently could not have cared less about Stuart doctrines of divine right and passive obedience. He believed that in extreme cases overthrowing a monarch was necessary. "If a sovereign oppresses his people to a great degree, they will rise up and cut off his head."[58] This appeal to the exigencies of "human nature," as he called it, recurs both in his recorded conversation and in his writings. It might well help to explain his meaning of "necessity" with reference to the Revolution of 1688; James had crossed the threshold of tolerance and was dethroned by his people through a necessary reflex of human nature. "It was become impossible," he said, "for him to reign any longer in this country."[59] At the same time, the Revolution "broke the constitution." Johnson set great store in the belief that reverence for the monarch, and by extension government, constituted the very heart of civil order. In the Vinerian law lectures that he helped to write, the king is called "the political soul" of parliament and of the nation.[60] Amidst the turbulent 1770s and early 1780s, when even Burke alleged that tyranny was worse than in the days of James II, when conflicting interpretations of the Revolution fueled both public riots and calls for wholesale constitutional change, Johnson feared the use of the Revolution of 1688 to foment dangerous discontent. In a lifetime of writing, he refused to celebrate this Revolution as a constitutional precedent or to express unqualified hatred of James, whom he nonetheless blamed for his own fate. He accepted the need for the Revolution and, to quote Charles Davenant again, acknowledged that this event had produced "good." He was also too cautious a political observer, and too skeptical of vagaries incident to historical recall, to underwrite an assessment of the Revolution that justified the right of the people to overthrow a monarch which it disliked. Such an interpretation, he believed, amounted to a recipe for chaos.[61]

58   Ibid., 2:170. See also Johnson's sermon on the day commemorating the execution of Charles I (January 30), where he comments on the legality of resisting "such insolence as may be restrained, and such oppression as may be lawfully resisted": Sermon 23, in Samuel Johnson, *Sermons*, in *The Yale Edition of the Works of Samuel Johnson*, eds. Jean Hagstrum and James Gray, vol. 14 (New Haven and London: Yale University Press), 243–244. For discussion of this sermon in its context, see Howard D. Weinbrot, "The Thirtieth of January Sermon: Swift, Johnson, Sterne, and the Evolution of Culture," *Eighteenth-Century Life* 34 (2010): 29–55.

59   *Boswell's Life*, 1:430.

60   Chambers and Johnson, *Course of Lectures*, 1:138.

61   Johnson's well-known remark that a people, if greatly oppressed, will be impelled to cut off the sovereign's head cannot, in my view, be taken as an indication of political liberalism. In response to radical and dissenting calls for incremental innovations to the establishment, conservative authors frequently argued like Johnson that "nature" provided an ultimate safeguard against severe oppression. See my *Samuel Johnson and Eighteenth-Century Thought* (Oxford: Clarendon Press, 1988), 247-251, where I compare Johnson's statement

Hence the supposed inconsistencies that I noted earlier, his habit of alternately endorsing the Revolution yet refusing to embark on Whiggish expostulations on the power of the people and the tyranny of the Stuarts. Johnson feared the restive and envious nature of human beings, which he saw all too well demonstrated by the electors of Middlesex and by the patriots of America. While I do not implicitly trust Boswell's assessments of Johnson, the following statement strikes me as a fair summary of what Johnson probably thought, and which Boswell may have learned from him: "The Revolution was *necessary*, but not a subject for *glory*; because it for a long time blasted the generous feelings of *Loyalty*. And now, when by the benignant effect of time the present Royal Family are established in our *affections*, how unwise it is to revive by celebrations the memory of a shock, which it would surely have been better that our constitution had not required."[62]

This seems a good synopsis, but there remains one further question which might be considered highly speculative. It is, nonetheless, a very interesting question and one which might help to put Johnson's attitudes into historical perspective. How would Johnson have reacted to the French Revolution had he lived only five years more?

Johnson knew some of the principal actors who would dominate the English political stage during the 1790s. He knew Charles James Fox, who emerged as a notorious booster of the French Revolution, finding a new podium in his vaunted role as "the Man of the People" during Johnson's lifetime. Interestingly, Johnson liked Fox, who belonged to the Club. When Fox was campaigning against the king's new prime minister, the young William Pitt, in the historic 1784 election, Johnson said that "I am for the King against Fox; but I am for Fox against Pitt." In the face of Boswell's evident surprise at this opinion, Johnson explained, "Yes, Sir; the King is my master; but I do not know Pitt; and Fox is my friend." As Boswell commented, Johnson may have come to like the younger Pitt if he had lived a little longer, for this prime minister skillfully restored faith in government and reverence for the monarchy, even with the onset of George III's porphyria. Johnson and Pitt, moreover, shared important principles such as hatred of slavery and sympathy for Irish Catholics. But the future admirer of Jacobins, Fox, was equally no "low-born railer." He was, amazingly, the great-great-grandson of Charles II, by his mistress the Duchess of Portsmouth, and shared much of his ancestor's popular

in 1772 to arguments in two contemporary publications of a conservative cast, John Rotherham's *An Essay on Establishments in Religion* (Newcastle upon Tyne: J. White and T. Saint, 1767) and John Bellward's *The Established Mode of Subscription Vindicated* (Norwich: William Chase, 1774). See also the argument of Tobias Smollett's high Tory character, Mr. Jolter, in defense of French absolutism in *The Adventures of Peregrine Pickle* (1751), ed. James L. Clifford (London: Oxford University Press, 1964), chap. 47, 231–232.

62   *Boswell's Life*, 4:171, n. 1.

charisma. With typical enthusiasm for this talent, Johnson pronounced Fox "a most extraordinary man." He had "divided the Kingdom with Caesar; so that it was a doubt whether the nation should be ruled by the scepter of George the Third, or the tongue of Fox."[63] While also inheriting a Carolean passion for wine, women and gambling, inclinations that never much troubled Johnson, Fox was an accomplished classical scholar and shared his love for the Italian Renaissance. Johnson's liking for Fox at least shows that he did not despise even Whig populism when combined with real talent and intelligence.

That other "extraordinary man" in Johnson's company, Edmund Burke, came deeply to distrust Fox, his old ally among the Rockingham Whigs. For many years, Burke and Fox had appealed to that most elusive abstraction in late-century political rhetoric, the will of the "people." By the "people," the Rockingham Whigs presumably meant men of property like themselves. Yet even Burke, so linked to aristocratic interests, had allowed the inference that by the "people" he meant everyone in Great Britain. After the news of the French Revolution, Burke cleared his throat and began to throw scorn on the idea that he had ever meant the pike-wielding washerwomen and laborers who marched Louis XVI from Versailles to the Tuilleries. Fox, Burke implied, was no more a "Man of the People" than his friend and former lover the Duchess of Devonshire; on the part of this elite set, Jacobin populism was little more than hypocritical and irresponsible swaggering.[64] Burke also became alarmed by misinterpretations of the Revolution of 1688. In November 1789, the longtime radical Richard Price, a dissenting minister, preached a sermon entitled *A Discourse on the Love of our Country*. In this sermon, Price claimed that the Revolution had bestowed on the people the right "to choose our own governors" and generally to elect kings as they saw fit.[65] This perpetuated an old radical reading of 1688 enunciated in an even more extreme form by Catherine Macaulay. According to this doctrine, the Revolution was, at best, unfinished business, a business finished only, as Condorcet would claim, by the revolutionaries in France.

Opposing this misreading, Burke launched his famous *Reflections on the Revolution in France*, which begins by setting the record straight on what the English Revolution actually meant. As late as 1777, in a defiant "Address to the King," Burke had entertained the verbiage that the Revolution affirmed "the free choice . . . of the people."[66] In the face of radical patriotism so famously recalled by Wordsworth in *The Prelude*, he

---

63   *Boswell's Life*, 4:292.

64   On Burke's split with Fox, see F.P. Lock, *Edmund Burke*, 2 vols. (Oxford: Clarendon Press, 1988–2006), 2:256–258. Burke's consternation about the hypocrisy of British aristocrats supporting the French Revolution is most pungently advanced in his response to the Whig Duke of Bedford, *Letter to a Noble Lord*, in *Writings and Speeches*, 9:174–175.

65   Richard Price, *A Discourse on the Love of our Country* (London: G. Stafford, 1789).

66   *Writings and Speeches*, 3:273–274.

now reverted to the argument that the Revolution represented at best "a small and a temporary deviation from the strict order of a regular hereditary succession."[67] The overriding goal of the noble and learned men who had engineered the Revolution had been "that they might not relax the nerves of their monarchy."[68] The events of the Revolution of 1688 had been precipitated by an "extreme emergency."[69] In Burke's *Reflections*, the English "people" were no longer the discontented and potentially revolutionary lot imagined in the *Thoughts on the Cause of the Present Discontents*. They were now a majority who revered the king and even the King's Friends. They loved the aristocracy, which Burke had always supported, but also the Church of England, which had never figured much in his writings and speeches.

I agree with F.P. Lock and others that *Reflections on the Revolution in France* signals no fundamental transformation in Burke's thought.[70] It is rather a coming clean, a clearing of hot air. Burke had probably always thought more or less what he confessed in this treatise, though he had been previously deceived by the sound of a discontented rhetoric fashionable in the 1770s. These were the days of Burke's friendship with Johnson, whose opinions Burke surely recalled. Each of the positions that I have just picked out from the *Reflections* bears a strong resemblance to what Johnson had long maintained, particularly the view that the Revolution was a deviation from heredity justified only by extreme necessity, and that upholding veneration for the king was of crucial political importance. The parallel is far from exact. Johnson had never thought that the English people were particularly loyal or respectful of their social superiors, particularly in the wake of 1688. In *The Patriot* (1774), Johnson called the "people" a "very heterogeneous and confused mass of the wealthy and the poor, the wise and the foolish, the good and the bad."[71] They could not be easily amalgamated under an overarching cultural generalization, and needed the authority of strong laws and strong kingship to keep them in order. Nevertheless, the older Burke may well have remembered his friend's warnings about evoking the specter of Revolution and seeding discontent against the king. Johnson would have been on Burke's side in the 1790s, but he would have regretted that his own prognosis needed to be so urgently reaffirmed. Johnson's political outlook may not be particularly amenable to attitudes in our own

---

67 *Reflections on the Revolution in France*, in ibid., 8:68.

68 Ibid., 8:70.

69 Ibid., 8:72.

70 As Lock points out, Burke's *Appeal from the Old to the New Whigs* (1791) represents a defense of his own "consistency," contrary to the widespread charge that he had become more "conservative." Burke regarded himself as a "uniform Whig." See Lock, *Edmund Burke*, 2: 379–390. See also John Brewer, *Party Ideology and Popular Politics at the Accession of George III* (Cambridge: Cambridge University Press, 1976), 238–239.

71 *Political Writings*, 10:394

time, either right or left. While shaped by his historical experience, however, the following formulation of his views makes abiding sense: social order and the avoidance of revolution rely on the maintenance of public institutions that instill respect and ensure a broad social consensus.

Johnson and Slavery

James G. Basker

URING A SABBATICAL YEAR IN 1993–94, I noticed for the first time a strange footnote in the first edition of Boswell's *Life of Johnson* (1791) that piqued my interest in the question of Johnson and slavery.[1] When I discussed it with Walter Jackson Bate a few weeks later, he offered energetic encouragement, which helped decide me to pursue the subject in depth.[2] A few essays followed and evolved into a book-length project on which I am now working, under the title *Samuel Johnson, Abolitionist: The Story Boswell Never Told*.[3] The rationale for that subtitle will become self-evident, I hope, in the course of this essay. I propose to illuminate selected moments in Johnson's lifelong opposition to slavery, particularly those that are minimized or missing altogether in Boswell's *Life of Johnson*. Ultimately, I want to offer a new angle of vision on Johnson, one that does a couple of things for us as students of his life and work.

The first is to make us aware of the degree to which Boswell, who was active as a pro-slavery advocate in the abolition debates of the times, shaped and delimited our perception of Johnson on this issue. As strange as it may sound, we all need to reread Boswell's *Life* as in part a pro-slavery text, a book that at certain points subordinates Johnson's views on slavery to Boswell's own pro-slavery position. The second is to enable us to see, in an era in which it can seem that everyone supported, or at least acquiesced in, the existence of racial slavery, that an eminent white writer and pillar of the establishment like Johnson could emerge as an ardent and persistent opponent of slavery. As we reassemble and explore the evidence, it becomes remarkable that

1   I am grateful to the Master and Fellows of Sidney Sussex College, Cambridge, and to the English Department at Harvard for their generous support during that sabbatical year.

2   Like many Johnsonians, including those at the "Johnson at 300" Conference at Harvard's Houghton Library, where an earlier version of this paper was presented, I am forever indebted to Jack Bate for his scholarship and teaching, as well as his personal encouragement.

3   The earlier essays include: "Samuel Johnson and the African-American Reader," *The New Rambler: Journal of the Johnson Society of London* Serial DX (1995): 47–57; "'The Next Insurrection': Johnson, Race, and Rebellion," *The Age of Johnson* 11 (2000): 37–51; "Intimations of Abolitionism in 1759: Johnson, Hawkesworth, and *Oroonoko*," *The Age of Johnson* 12 (2001): 47–66; "Multicultural Perspectives: Johnson, Race, and Gender," in *Johnson Re-Visioned: Looking Before and After*, ed. Philip Smallwood (Lewisburg: Bucknell University Press, 2001), 64–79; "Johnson, Boswell, and the Abolition of Slavery," *The New Rambler: Journal of the Johnson Society of London* Serial EV (2002): 36–48.

Johnson, who had never spent a single moment in Africa or in any of the slave-holding colonies, could nonetheless have had his life and writing touched so deeply by slavery—and yet our inherited image of him, until recently, could exhibit so few signs of that impact.

Let me start by revisiting two episodes that *are* mentioned in Boswell.

One night in 1769, Johnson went to dinner in his college in Oxford—not Pembroke, where he had begun in 1728, but University College, with which he had begun a new and vital relationship in 1761. He walked with his host, the young Vinerian Professor of Law Robert Chambers (1737–1803), from Chambers's professorial residence at New Inn Hall, where Johnson was staying, down High Street to University College, where Chambers was a Fellow and Johnson had become by the late 1760s a regular guest. Arriving in the College dining hall, they joined the usual cohort of a dozen fellows and one or two guests. The fellows ranged in seniority from the engaging but eccentric John Coulson (1719–1788), a member of the college since 1744, to the brilliant young scholar William Scott, later Lord Stowell (1745–1836), who had been appointed a fellow just four years earlier, at the age of twenty. Dinner at High Table was presided over by the master, Johnson's good friend Nathan Wetherell (1726–1807), who had also recently begun a four-year term as vice chancellor of Oxford University. Wearing his black academic gown, taking his seat next to the master, conversing familiarly with everyone at the table, Johnson seemed more like a fellow of the college himself than a guest. Indeed, Johnson had been spending a lot of time in the college in recent years: between 1767 and 1769 he made at least seven visits to "Univ," as it is called by Oxonians, twice staying in residence for more than two months at a stretch.[4] No wonder that when he was helping the son of his friend William Strahan gain admission to Univ in the 1760s, Johnson assured him of the strength of his connections: "The College is almost filled with my friends."[5]

That evening, the conversation flowed over everything from college gossip to politics and culture, gaining energy as the wine went round, and rising to yet another level as the group moved to the Senior Common Room for more drinks and dessert.[6] At some point, the conversation turned to recent news from the colonies: the *Gentleman's Magazine* (June 1769) carried a report from Jamaica that the black mistress of a white merchant, catching wind "of a conspiracy among the negroes of Kingston," had tipped off the authorities, enabling the militia to intercept "a force of 300 armed negroes"

---

4   Johnson visited University College twelve times between 1762 and 1770, including these seven visits in the period 1767–69: March–April 1767, May 1767, October 1767, February–April 1768, December 1768, February 1769, and May–August 1769.

5   Johnson to William Strahan, October 24, 1764, *The Letters of Samuel Johnson*, ed. Bruce Redford, 5 vols. (Princeton: Princeton University Press, 1992), 1: 245 (hereafter cited as *Letters of Samuel Johnson*).

6   The Senior Common Room Johnson knew is today called the "Winter Common Room," where there still hangs (as of July 2009) an engraving of Johnson donated and signed by William Scott in 1785.

whose aim had been to set fire to the city, kill all the whites, and spread rebellion across the whole of the island. The hair-raising tale ended happily, at least from one point of view: the plot had been prevented, and the leaders executed.[7] But mention of this story prompted others, and there was considerable back-and-forth about various uprisings and plots and bloody reprisals in the news during the past year: in Senegal and Gambia on the African coast (July 1769), in Montserrat (June 1768) and Dutch Guiana (March 1769) in the Caribbean, and even Boston, Massachusetts (October 1769) and Alexandria, Virginia (March 1768) on the North American mainland. Someone remembered a detail of the Virginia insurrection, as reported in the *Gentleman's Magazine*, that the negro rebels had "been executed, their heads cut off, and fixed on the chimnies of the court house [in Alexandria]."[8] Someone else opined that however barbaric and brutal slavery was overseas, the institution was also corrupting public morality in England itself, citing a story from a few months earlier about a gentleman who came to England and, short of money, sold his seventeen-year-old female slave (described in the press as "a very agreeable negro girl") for thirty guineas.[9]

This grim discussion was interrupted by Master Wetherell, who called the assemblage to order and raised his glass. Around the room, fellow by fellow, one witty and clever toast followed another, laughter and cheers broke out, and the atmosphere became playful and tipsy, as it normally was on these evenings.[10] At last came Johnson's turn. He rose and, seemingly intent on puncturing the lighthearted mood, thundered out "Here's to the *next* insurrection of the negroes in the West Indies." After a moment's silence, several in the room responded with a low-voiced "hear, hear." Conversation resumed, but the evening was winding down and soon ended. Johnson and Chambers took their leave and walked back to New Inn Hall where Frank Barber, a former slave from Jamaica, and now Johnson's beloved servant and surrogate son, helped Johnson prepare for bed. Before going to sleep that night, Johnson and Frank, as was their practice, knelt and prayed together. Perhaps that evening, thinking of Frank and the horrors of Jamaica he had escaped as a child, Johnson prayed with even more fervor than usual.

Students of Johnson and Boswell will recognize that in my rendering of this episode, I have fleshed it out with details—most of them historically accurate, all of them plausible—that dramatize the difference between it and Boswell's version in the

7 *Gentleman's Magazine* 39 (June 1769): 317–318.

8 Ibid., 38 (March 1768): 141.

9 Ibid., 38 (December 1768): 585.

10 For an example of the banter and wit that is known to have characterized a late-night common room drinking session that Johnson was involved in at Cambridge in 1765, see Basker, "Dictionary Johnson Amidst the Dons of Sidney: A Chapter in Eighteenth-Century Cambridge History," *Sidney Sussex College, Cambridge: Historical Essays in Commemoration of the Quatercentenary*, ed. D. E. D. Beales and H. B. Nisbet (Woodbridge, Suffolk: Boydell Press, 1996), 134–138.

Life, which consists of a single sentence. Boswell writes: "Upon one occasion, when in company with some very grave men at Oxford, his toast was, 'Here's to the next insurrection of the Negroes in the West Indies.'"[11] How little Boswell tells us, and how much he might have, if he had investigated and elaborated this intriguing episode with the same thoroughness he usually displayed. Surely he could tell us his source for the story, probably someone who was there? And from that source did he not learn—or did he decide to withhold from his readers?—the name of the college where it took place, the year, the names of others who were present, how they reacted, what else was said, *any* of the other circumstances? Including, for example, how often Johnson had publicly condoned violence by slaves against their masters, from the *Life of Drake* in 1740–1741 to *Taxation No Tyranny* (1775) thirty five years later? Or the fact that slave insurrections were so common in the eighteenth century that in the three dozen years from 1737 to 1773, the *Gentleman's Magazine* carried fifty-two articles covering forty-three different slave insurrections, insurrections that occurred from the African coast across the Atlantic to the Caribbean, and up and down the Americas? No one in the room, no literate person anywhere, could have been unaware or indifferent to the frequency and bloodiness of slave insurrections.[12] Moreover, in later years Boswell surely knew that Johnson's Oxford friends Wetherell, Coulson, Scott, and several others were alive and available for questioning throughout the time he was drafting and revising the *Life of Johnson* and, had he wished, he could have gathered every detail of the story behind Johnson's anti-slavery toast from them.

Or is it possible that Boswell forewent all these avenues because he had no interest in elaborating the scene or explaining Johnson's toast, preferring instead to present it as an outrageous outburst by a character he was shaping in his narrative: Johnson the volatile contrarian, Johnson the conversational performer? Why else would Boswell add the quasi-comical detail, that Johnson's audience that night were some "very grave men of Oxford," when in fact the college fellows were mostly energetic young men in their twenties and more prone to uproarious, drunken behavior, than gravity? If we look at the preceding sentence, we notice that Johnson's anti-slavery toast is actually presented as an illustrative proof of Boswell's main contention, that Johnson had always been "very zealous against slavery" but that his was a "zeal without knowledge."[13] If we zoom back a bit further, we begin to see that Boswell has embedded Johnson's slave insurrection toast within a fuller account of another slavery-related story, which, as it turns out, is the second episode I want to discuss.

11   *Boswell's Life of Johnson, Together with Boswell's Journal of a Tour to the Hebrides and Johnson's Diary of a Journal into North Wales*, ed. George Birkbeck Hill, rev. L. F. Powell, 6 vols. (Oxford: Clarendon Press, 1934–1950, rev. 1971), 3:200. All further citations are to this edition of *Boswell's Life* unless otherwise noted.

12   For details, see Basker, "'The Next Insurrection': Johnson, Race, and Rebellion," 39–43.

13   *Boswell's Life*, 3:200.

For this one, Boswell does give us a specific setting and date: Ashbourne, September 23, 1777. Boswell had joined Johnson on a two-week visit to his friend John Taylor's house in Ashbourne and he writes about that visit in the *Life* in considerable detail. On his final night with Johnson, which fell on September 23, Boswell got Johnson to dictate a memo about a court case in Scotland that he wanted to carry back with him to Edinburgh the next day. This case had been going on for three years, involved a large cast of characters connected with Johnson, and was of profound historic significance in settling once and for all the legal status of racial slavery in Scotland. But one gets none of that from Boswell. Instead, even as he begins to tell a story that might *dramatize* Johnson's anti-slavery activism, Boswell contrives to minimize and obscure it. Boswell's pervasive narrative control deserves closer examination.

The first detail to notice is that up until this point in the *Life*, page 174 of the second volume, two-thirds of the way through the biography, with Johnson entering his sixty-ninth year, no mention has been made whatsoever of slavery or of Johnson's views on the subject; nor have the words "slave" or "slavery" been allowed to appear anywhere in the text. Even when introducing Francis Barber hundreds of pages earlier (1: 128, 130), Boswell had avoided using the words "slavery" or "slave" at all, preferring instead the more euphemistic term "servant."[14] (We will turn to Francis Barber's story in a minute.) At this moment in 1777, Johnson is sixty-eight years old, and he is about to dictate a memorandum for a court case that would decide whether a Jamaican slave now living in Scotland was entitled to his freedom. It is here, in a single paragraph of eight sentences, that Boswell first introduces the topic of slavery into the *Life of Johnson*:

> After supper I accompanied him to his apartment, and at my request he dictated to me an argument in favour of the negro who was then claiming his liberty, in an action in the Court of Session in Scotland. He had always been very zealous against slavery in every form, in which I with all deference thought that he discovered 'a zeal without knowledge.' Upon one occasion, when in company with some very grave men at Oxford, his toast was, "Here's to the next insurrection of the negroes in the West-Indies." His violent prejudice against our West-Indian and American settlers appeared whenever there was an opportunity. Towards the conclusion of his 'Taxation no Tyranny,' he says, "how is it that we hear the loudest *yelps* for liberty among the drivers of negroes?" and in his conversation with Mr. Wilkes, he asked, "Where did Beckford and Trecothick learn English?" That Trecothick could speak and write good English is well known. I myself was favoured with his correspondence concerning the brave Corsicans. And that Beckford could speak it with a spirit of honest

14   All volume and page references in this paragraph are to the first edition: James Boswell, *The Life of Samuel Johnson, LL.D.*, 2 vols. (London: Charles Dilly, 1791).

resolution even to his Majesty, as his 'faithful Lord-Mayor of London,' is commemorated by the noble monument erected to him in Guildhall.[15]

The compression and sequencing are masterful, and Boswell's rhetorical skill here accomplishes a great deal.

The first sentence, for example, reduces a major saga into a few words that tell us almost nothing. The unidentified "negro" is Joseph Knight, whose character and behavior reveal him as an extraordinarily heroic, if forgotten, man. Joseph had fallen in love with a white servant girl, Ann Thomson; she had become pregnant; their master John Wedderburn fired her; Joseph asked for wages or permission to work off the estate so he could support her and the baby; the master denied every request; Joseph ran away but was apprehended and returned; meanwhile, the baby was born but died ten days later; Joseph managed to sneak away to Perth and file a petition for his freedom in the Sheriff's Court which, after two denials, was granted on the third try; he rejoined Ann in Edinburgh, where they married and soon had another baby; meanwhile Wedderburn the master appealed the sheriff's decision all the way to the Court of Session in Edinburgh, where the lawyer John Maclaurin, a friend of both Boswell and Johnson, represented Joseph *gratis* for more than three years.[16] Even this summary is barebones. The larger tapestry of Joseph Knight's story has bits of everything: the Jacobite rebellion of 1745, the ordeal of the middle passage, gothic scenes in Scottish castles and Caribbean plantations, interracial love, illegitimate children, a treacherous master, a kindly priest, escape and recapture, a tense courtroom drama, a thrilling outcome. There were fifteen eminent justices hearing the case, five of them friends or acquaintances of Johnson's, as were several of the lawyers involved. The case had monumental legal significance for Scotland and, potentially, for much of the English-speaking world. Yet none of this gets a whisper or a wink from Boswell: he terms it merely "an action in the Court of Session."

The cryptic opening sentence is in any case immediately subsumed by the second: "He had always been very zealous against slavery in every form, in which I with all deference thought that he discovered 'a zeal without knowledge.'" This is Boswell's thesis sentence for the paragraph, the logic of which retroactively transforms Johnson's dictation of a memo "in favour of the negro" into just the first of several instances that prove Johnson's zealous ignorance about the subject of slavery. Boswell offers four more instances in the next three sentences: Johnson's toast "to the next insurrection of the negroes," his "violent prejudice" against white West-Indians and Americans, his anti-American complaints about hearing "the loudest *yelps* for liberty among the drivers of negroes," and his dismissive comments to John Wilkes, who Boswell forgets to mention was also an opponent of slavery, about the poor English spoken by men

---

15   Boswell, *Life of Samuel Johnson*, 2:174.

16   See Basker, "Johnson, Boswell, and the Abolition of Slavery," 42–46.

from slave-holding colonies such as William Beckford (who was from such a colony) and Barlow Trecothick (who was not).

All these Boswell presents as pretty obvious proof that on the subject of slavery Johnson was irrational and uninformed. Boswell laces the section with language that subliminally reinforces the sense of Johnson as slightly unhinged: "zealous" and "zeal without knowledge" were terms reserved in the eighteenth century for the lunatic fringe, and "insurrections," "violent prejudice" and "yelps" only compound the sense of lunacy. By the sixth sentence of the paragraph, the topic of slavery has vanished, as if Johnson's irrationality on the subject was so firmly proven, really to the point of embarrassment, that Boswell could readily change the subject. He rounds things off with some fulsome compliments to Beckford, shamelessly invoking even the king for support, while slyly allowing the topic of slavery to disappear completely.

As if he had not done enough in that paragraph to undermine and discredit Johnson's opposition to slavery, Boswell took a further step. Instead of printing the text of Johnson's "argument in favor of the negro," Boswell here in the first edition of the *Life* acknowledged its absence and inserted an apologetic footnote: "This being laid up somewhere amidst my multiplicity of papers at Auchinleck, has escaped my search for this work; but, when found, I shall take care that my readers shall have it."[17] This is the strange and arresting footnote that I mentioned in the beginning. Boswell's faltering grammar ("but, when found, I shall . . .") suggests that indeed it is he, as much as the document, that is a bit lost. As I have argued elsewhere, it seems clear that Boswell deliberately left it out. He omitted—or at least conveniently misplaced—the document that contains the most trenchant and forceful argument Johnson ever wrote against slavery, one that helped to win a high court case, gain a slave his freedom, and end forever the institution of slavery in Scotland.[18]

The evidence is circumstantial but, I think, persuasive. This is the only place in the entire *Life* where Boswell says that he has a Johnson document but cannot print it because it is lost in his files. Moreover, Boswell had ample opportunity over the years he was drafting and revising the *Life* to go find the Knight document, or send someone to dig it out, or even to obtain the text from others such as his close friend John Maclaurin, who represented Joseph Knight in court throughout the trial and had his own copy of it. Though Boswell's correspondence shows him in the final months of preparation scurrying around to gather and include new materials, and to check or correct other passages in his magnum opus, there is no evidence he made any effort to recover the Knight brief by any of these means. Meanwhile, in the very months he was proofing the sheets of the *Life*, Boswell had also been writing and arranging to publish his own pamphlet in *defense* of the slave trade, the embarrassing twenty-four-page

17   Boswell, *Life of Samuel Johnson*, 2:174.

18   Basker, "Johnson, Boswell, and the Abolition of Slavery," 42–48.

poetic harangue entitled *No Abolition of Slavery*.[19] He timed its publication carefully to influence the long-awaited Parliamentary debate over Wilberforce's abolition bill which had been grinding through Parliament for two years. "I am thinking to curtail my poem on the Slave Trade," he wrote to his friend William Temple on April 2, 1791, "and throw it into the world just before the great question comes on next Wednesday."[20] With tactical precision, Boswell's anti-abolition pamphlet was published on April 16, two days before debate on the abolition bill began in Parliament on April 18.[21]

The complexities of that debate and its outcome are beyond the scope of this essay, but a couple of details are noteworthy. First, one of Boswell's earliest and most avid readers was William Wilberforce, who took up the *Life* as soon as it came out in May 1791, reading it every morning over breakfast and becoming so engrossed on some mornings that he was almost late to Parliament during the critical summer of 1791.[22] As a result of Boswell's omission, Wilberforce did not, *could* not, read the arguments against slavery that Johnson had expounded successfully in the Joseph Knight case in 1777. Who now can say what Wilberforce and his allies might have accomplished in 1791 if they had been able to enlist Johnson's arguments, his voice and reputation, in their efforts? Who can say if it might in any way have altered or mitigated the outcome of the parliamentary debate, which saw Wilberforce's abolition bill shelved in 1791, then compromised and effectively defeated in 1792, delaying for more than fifteen years the abolition of the slave trade, until January 1, 1808?[23] Who can say whether what we in our literary studies see as textual issues of composition and interpretation, might actually

19   [James Boswell], *No Abolition of Slavery; Or the Universal Empire of Love* (London: Printed for R. Faulder, 1791). Boswell privately distributed copies to his friends and acknowledged his authorship publicly in a biographical sketch of himself that he placed (anonymously) in the *European Magazine and London Review* 19 (May and June 1791): 407. According to a note in the Boswell manuscripts at Yale, his friend John Courtenay contributed six lines to the poem; see Basker, *Amazing Grace: An Anthology of Poems About Slavery 1660–1810* (New Haven: Yale University Press, 2002), 239 and note.

20   Boswell to the Reverend William Temple, April 2, 1791, *Letters of James Boswell*, ed. Chauncey Brewster Tinker, 2 vols. (Oxford: Clarendon Press, 1924), 2: 433.

21   *The Correspondence of James Boswell with Certain Members of the Club*, ed. Charles N. Fifer (New York: McGraw-Hill, 1976), Appendix 1, 418, notes 1 and 2.

22   See John Pollock, *Wilberforce* (London: Constable, 1977), 43.

23   Historians have estimated that when Wilberforce first introduced his abolition bill in 1789, only about thirty-five MPs were committed to abolishing slavery, and the same number to preserving it at all costs, leaving roughly 488 of the 558 members of Parliament yet to be decided and presumably open to persuasion. See William Hague, *William Wilberforce: The Life of the Great Anti-Slave Trade Campaigner* (London: Harcourt, 2007), 169–170, 197–198, and 259–260. Over the years 1791 to 1796 Wilberforce would repeatedly introduce abolition bills and repeatedly lose, by as much as 163–88 in one vote and as little as 74–70 in another.

have had some real impact in the world, might have contributed in some small way to political decisions and events that affected the lives of millions of people?

One person who did regard Johnson's anti-slavery legal brief as potentially influential, and therefore dangerous, was Boswell himself, as we can see from the way he treated the text when he finally published it. Having allowed the second printing of the *Life* to go forward without it in 1793, Boswell included it instead in the "Addenda" that were printed afterwards and then inserted as part of the prefatory material. Even with Johnson's text buried in the "Addenda" to the second edition, which were probably passed over and ignored by the vast majority of readers, Boswell could not resist including his own rebuttal to Johnson's attack on slavery that is almost as long as the original itself—fifty lines of his text, to Johnson's sixty one.[24] Boswell could not let it rest. It was only after Boswell's death, with Malone's carefully revised third edition of the *Life* in 1799, that ordinary readers could find and read within the text of the *Life* itself Johnson's long-suppressed anti-slavery legal brief.[25]

Having urged the need for us to be a bit more skeptical in reading Boswell on the slavery question, I would like now to set Boswell aside, to focus on some moments in Johnson's life itself. Johnson expressed his antipathy to slavery several times between his arrival in London in 1738 and his completion of the *Rambler* in 1752: in his *Life of Drake* (1740–1741), the *Life of Savage* (1744), some lines in the first draft of *Vanity of Human Wishes* which were later deleted (c. 1748–1749), his editorial revisions of William Dodd's poem "The African Prince" (1749) for the *Gentleman's Magazine*, perhaps even in the editorial work of selecting and submitting to the *Gentleman's Magazine* occasional news stories about slave rebellions picked up from newspapers and other sources.[26] Johnson's attitude and beliefs were evident from early on, but his sense of slavery changed profoundly in the spring of 1752, when Francis Barber entered his life. From that day, slavery as an idea gave way to the tangible reality of one of its

24   James Boswell, *The Life of Samuel Johnson LL.D.*, [2nd ed.] 2 vols. (London: Charles Dilly, 1793), 1:ix [misprint for xiv]-xviii.

25   See *Boswell's Life*, 3:201–205. In a later section of the *Life*, Boswell had also written a short report on the outcome of the case, which was a vote of 10–4 in favor of Knight and the end of slavery in Scotland. But his account is convoluted and slanted against Knight, and ends bizarrely with a reaffirmation of the legal and historical justifications for slavery as a legitimate institution, "which," writes Boswell, "has been acknowledged in all ages and countries, and that when freedom flourished, as in old Greece and Rome." See *Boswell's Life*, 3:212–214.

26   Basker, "Johnson, Boswell, and the Abolition of Slavery," 37–44. No serious study has yet been done of the articles in the *Gentleman's Magazine* that deal with slavery, yet such material permeates the magazine, appearing several times a year throughout the eighteenth century.

victims standing in front of him, a little black child from Jamaica who would be part of his family for the next thirty-two years.

The basic elements of Francis Barber's story were first laid out by Aleyn Lyell Reade in his *Johnsonian Gleanings* in 1912 and then augmented and retold in various accounts, including Lyle Larsen's *Dr. Johnson's Household* (1985) and Gretchen Gerzina's *Black London: Life Before Emancipation* (1995).[27] But the inclination to ignore Barber and his place in Johnson's life, or to efface him altogether, persisted as well. In the 1950s, the same decade in which Ralph Ellison's revolutionary novel *Invisible Man* appeared, the eminent Johnsonian Bertrand Bronson published a one-volume collection of Johnson's works in which he included a two-page chronology of Johnson's life and writings, and an original eight-page introductory essay on Johnson. In neither the chronology nor the introduction is Francis Barber even mentioned, and because this volume, twice revised, remained a staple of college course book sales through the 1960s and 1970s, many thousands of college graduates would be forgiven for not knowing that Francis Barber even existed, or that a black man figured centrally in Johnson's consciousness for more than thirty years.[28] For a time, Francis was in danger of becoming the invisible man in Johnson's life. There still remains a great deal to do before we recover a full sense of Francis Barber the person and his relationship with Johnson, a gap that fiction writers and playwrights have discerned and attempted to remedy, with varying degrees of success.[29] I want to focus here on questions arising from three periods in Frank's life, for which we might begin to formulate new and more satisfactory answers than we have had so far.

The first concern his childhood and his former life in Jamaica, and they touch on the most fundamental questions about any person's life: What are his origins? Who were his parents? Why was he brought to England in the first place? Hawkins, Boswell, and the other early biographers, and Francis himself, in some carefully worded statements he made to Boswell a few years after Johnson's death, give the basic account. He came with Colonel Richard Bathurst, father of Johnson's close friend the physician Richard Bathurst, from Jamaica to England as a young boy aged seven or eight at the end of 1749, arriving in England in early 1750. Colonel Bathurst took Francis to Lincoln, where

27   Aleyn Lyell Reade, "Francis Barber: The Doctor's Servant," *Johnsonian Gleanings*, Part 2 (1912, repr. New York: Octagon, 1968); Lyle Larsen, *Dr. Johnson's Household* (Hamden, Conn.: Archon, 1985); Gretchen Gerzina, *Black London: Life Before Emancipation* (New Brunswick, N.J.: Rutgers University Press, 1995).

28   Samuel Johnson, *Rasselas, Poems & Selected Prose*, ed. Bertrand H. Bronson (New York: Holt, Rinehart and Winston, 1958), vii–xiv and xvii–xviii. The same holds true of the revised editions of 1966 and 1971.

29   See, for example, John Wain, *Frank* (Oxford: Amber Lane Press, 1984); Darryl Pinckney, *High Cotton* (New York: Penguin, 1992); Dave Randle, *A Troublesome Disorder* (New Romney: Bank House Books, 2002); and Caryl Phillips, *Foreigners: Three English Lives* (New York: Knopf, 2007).

the Bathurst family had roots and Bathurst's son Richard was practicing medicine. Bathurst immediately placed Francis in a boarding school about thirty miles away in south Yorkshire, where he remained for most of two years. During this period Colonel Bathurst also inserted a clause in his will by which Francis would be freed upon his death. In 1752, just as Johnson suffered the death of his beloved Tetty, the Bathursts brought Francis to Johnson and, apparently moved by a mixture of concern for the grieving Johnson and solicitude for Francis's future, placed him in Johnson's custody forever.[30]

No one seems ever to have asked the most important though potentially embarrassing question: Why would Bathurst have brought Francis to England in the first place? The traditional account suggests he brought him as a servant. But a seven-year-old child is more of a dependent than a servant, and one does not bring a servant on a long and expensive transoceanic voyage only to place him in boarding school for two years. In the eighteenth century, colonial plantation owners brought individual slaves with them to Europe for various reasons: certainly they brought their favorite servants, their valets, their cooks, their children's nannies, their mistresses, sometimes even their elderly loyal retainers to be rewarded with emancipation, or an easier life. But Francis did not fit any of these categories. Besides, records show that in 1749 Colonel Bathurst had almost 150 slaves of all ages on his estate, the Orange River Plantation, on the north central coast of Jamaica.[31] Why take little Francis instead of any of them? In the post-Sally Hemings era of slavery studies, another answer suggests itself: Francis was very likely Colonel Bathurst's blood relative—his nephew, or grandson, or, most probably, his own son. Only a DNA test that links descendents of Bathurst and Barber will ever prove this for sure, but it is the answer that would explain so many of the pieces: the selection of one little boy to be salvaged from hundreds of slaves on a bankrupt plantation, which Bathurst had to sell in August 1749, the trouble taken to transport Francis to England and to educate him privately, the codicil in Bathurst's will to free him, even the care to place him with a guardian like Johnson who hated slavery and would protect him from ever being subjected to it again.

If Johnson guessed or knew this family secret, it would explain much more: Johnson's devotion to Frank, his generosity (some called it folly) in paying for Frank's education, his patience and forgiveness as Frank acted out his adolescence by repeatedly running away, his solicitude for Frank and his white wife and their children,

30   See *The Correspondence and Other Papers of James Boswell Relating to the Making of the Life of Johnson*, ed. Marshall Waingrow, 2nd ed. (Edinburgh: Edinburgh University Press; New Haven: Yale University Press, 2001), 127, and Sir John Hawkins, *The Life of Samuel Johnson, LL.D.*, ed. O M Brack Jr. (Athens: University of Georgia Press, 2009), 197–198.

31   Larsen, *Dr. Johnson's Household*, 25 and notes 7–9. Larsen's research raises the possibility that Francis's name before coming to England was Quashey, and that his mother may have been a slave woman named Grace, if his inferences from various Jamaican records are correct.

his passionate concern about Frank's religious education, his largess in bequeathing to Frank and his family the bulk of his estate when he died. A transfer of affection from his close friend Richard Bathurst to Frank would have intensified the attachment. In the years after Bathurst died, Johnson, according to those who knew him best, "hardly ever spoke of him without tears in his eyes."[32] Mrs. Piozzi quoted Johnson as calling him "my dear dear Bathurst, whom I loved better than ever I loved any human creature."[33] One of the reasons Johnson loved him is that Bathurst hated slavery too. According to Langton, Johnson remembered with "warm approbation" Bathurst saying "he was glad that his father . . . had left his affairs in total ruin, because having no estate, he was not under the temptation of having slaves."[34]

When little Francis came into Johnson's life in April 1752, he was not only the personification of the neglected and pitiable "negro child" that poets would make into a staple of sentimental literature in the second half of the eighteenth century. He was also, for Johnson, something of a surrogate for the child he and Tetty never had in their eighteen years of marriage, *and* the little brother or cousin of his dearest friend Richard Bathurst, bereft of family and entrusted to him for protection. Francis Barber embodied moral and familial obligation, supercharged with the emotions of loyalty, grief, love and pity—an overwhelmingly powerful combination for anyone, and especially for Johnson.

The next period of particular interest is Frank's adolescence, with the added strains it put on his relationship with Johnson and what has so long been overlooked, its connection with Johnson's writing. Modern scholarship has established that Frank ran away from home in the fall of 1756 and probably did not return to live in Johnson's house fulltime until August of 1760, though in the interim there were intervals of reconnection and warm relations.

The story falls into two segments, because Frank effectively ran away twice. The first time was in September 1756 when Frank, aged fourteen, full of the restlessness of apprentice-age boys, and upset over what in later life he described as "some difference" with Johnson, ran away without a trace. Johnson was understandably distressed. "My boy is run away," he wrote to his friend Lewis Paul in late September 1756.[35] Four months passed and Johnson had no idea where Frank was until in early 1757 he heard that Frank had been seen in Wapping, a waterfront area of London. Tellingly, Johnson's response was kindness, not anger. Rather than write him off or play the stern parent ("he'll be back when he realizes how good he had it"), Johnson placed this gently encouraging notice in the *Daily Advertiser* for February 14, 1757:

---

32   *Boswell's Life* 1:190, note 2.

33   Ibid.

34   Ibid., 4:28.

35   Johnson to Lewis Paul, Autumn [September] 1756, *Letters of Samuel Johnson*, 1:145.

Whereas Francis Barber, a black Boy, has been for some Months absent from his Master, and has been said to have lived lately in Wapping, or near it: This is to give him Notice, that if he will come to his Master, or apply to any of his Master's friends, he will be kindly received.[36]

Johnson was keen to bring Frank home again and, though he may have been mistaken about the Wapping location, his tactics seem to have succeeded. He and Frank were soon reconnected. As Frank himself reported to Boswell many years later, during his time away he had begun an apprenticeship with "a Mr. Farren Apothecary in Cheapside for about two years during which time he called some times on his Master [i.e., Johnson] and was well received."[37]

Relations between Johnson and Frank were much improved, and Frank told Boswell that soon he "was to return to" Johnson's service. At the last moment, Frank changed his mind. Instead, as Boswell reports Frank's explanation, "having an inclination to go to sea, he went accordingly." Here begins the second segment of Frank's time away, and a series of events that upset Johnson even more than the first time around. Frank disappeared and, unbeknownst to Johnson, joined the navy during the first week of June 1758. Johnson was distraught. For a long while he heard nothing. When he eventually learned that Frank had not been killed or kidnapped, but had enlisted in the navy, he was still so concerned that he appealed to a variety of people to help get Frank discharged, including his rival and sometime enemy Tobias Smollett, who had connections at the Admiralty Office. Responding to Johnson's pleas, Smollett wrote more than once to his contacts, including, on March 16, 1759, to John Wilkes. Although it would turn out otherwise, Smollett assumed, probably based on what Johnson told him, that Frank had been pressed into the navy. "I am again your Petitioner in behalf of that great Cham of Literature, Samuel Johnson," wrote Smollett. "His Black Servant, whose name is Francis Barber, has been pressed on board the Stag Frigate, Capt. Angel, and our Lexicographer is in great Distress."[38] Johnson's efforts continued for almost two years, with letters and appeals, until finally he succeeded in the summer of 1760, when Frank was discharged from the navy on August 8, after two years and two months of military service.

Looming in the background of both these episodes was the shadow of slavery. As Johnson knew, there were many things that could happen to a young black man in the streets of London in the 1750s—including at least one kind of danger that did not apply to white boys, that of being kidnapped or press-ganged, taken abroad, and sold as a slave.

36 Printed in Betty Rizzo, "The Elopement of Francis Barber," *English Language Notes* 23, no. 1 (1985): 36. As Professor Rizzo notes, Johnson's ad ran a second time on February 15.

37 *Correspondence of Boswell Relating to the Making of the Life*, 127.

38 Smollett to Wilkes, March 16, 1759, *The Letters of Tobias Smollett*, ed. Lewis M. Knapp (Oxford: Clarendon Press, 1970), 75.

At a time when slavery was legal everywhere in the English-speaking world (indeed, almost all the world), slaves had no civil rights and free blacks could scarcely count on the protection of the law either, whether in London or aboard a ship in the Royal Navy. In the 1760s, it would be a ruthless kidnapping that left a badly beaten fugitive slave to die in the streets that moved Granville Sharp to take up the cause, pursuing legal action on the slave's behalf that eventually resulted in the Somerset decision of 1772, which recognized limited rights of black slaves upon arrival in England and marked a turning point in the emerging fight against slavery.[39] Had Frank been kidnapped or beaten or sold abroad between 1758 and 1760, it might well have been Samuel Johnson rather than Granville Sharp who first pursued the legal protections for black people in England. It was this danger that Olaudah Equiano narrowly avoided for himself and witnessed others experiencing on several occasions in the 1760s and 1770s, aboard both commercial and naval ships, when free blacks were kidnapped and, beyond the reach of the law, sold into slavery.[40] It also was this danger, along with the ordinary peril of serving aboard a naval ship during wartime, that moved Johnson to persevere with parental intensity in getting Frank discharged from the navy, even if Frank didn't wish it.

What we have never done is to connect Johnson's experiences raising Frank with his life as a writer. It is exactly during this period 1756 to 1760 that the topic of slavery surfaces most frequently in his writings, often in brief eruptions that suggest anger welling up from within. Thus in 1756, in the first issue of the *Literary Magazine*, amidst a long critique of European colonialism and the Seven Years' War, Johnson interjects his memorable denunciation of Jamaica as "a place of great wealth and dreadful wickedness, a den of tyrants and a dungeon of slaves."[41] The same year, in what one would expect to be a routine preface he was hired to write for Richard Rolt's *A New Dictionary of Trade and Commerce*, we find Johnson suddenly flaring up and citing "the Traffick for Negroes" as the supreme example in all the world of a trade that, rather than being outlawed by statute, is "unlawful in itself."[42]

A couple of years later, when asked to write the introduction to a collection of voyages and discovery narratives called *The World Displayed*, Johnson devoted his thirty-page essay to a denunciation of the Portuguese conquest of Africa and especially of their development of the slave trade. Again, Johnson seems at times to boil over with

39   See Gerzina, *Black London*, 1–2.

40   Olaudah Equiano, *The Interesting Narrative and Other Writings*, ed. Vincent Carretta (New York: Penguin, 1995), 96–98 and 158–160.

41   "An Introduction to the Political State of Great Britain," *The Literary Magazine, or Universal Review*, 1 ([15 May], 1756): 4.

42   Preface to Richard Rolt, *A New Dictionary of Trade and Commerce* (London, 1756), quoted here from *Miscellaneous and Fugitive Pieces*, compiled and published by Thomas Davies, 3 vols. (London: Printed for T. Davies, 1774), 3:270.

personal anger about the subject. In one section, he becomes particularly incensed that the Portuguese seemed to regard the Africans as not even human. Though Johnson is discussing a period 200 years before the British involvement began, he contrives to connect this evil attitude of fifteenth-century Portuguese marauders with British slave owners of his own day. The Portuguese had no scruples about the cruel way they treated the Africans, he writes, "because they scarcely considered them as distinct from beasts; and indeed the practice of *all* the European nations, among others of the *English* barbarians that cultivate the southern islands of America proves, that this opinion, however absurd and foolish, however wicked and injurious, still continues to prevail."[43]

Throughout the essay, history fuels impassioned editorial comment as Johnson denounces European cruelty, treachery, and immorality toward the Africans, as part of a larger pattern of European imperialism: "The Europeans," Johnson concludes, "have scarcely visited any coast, but to gratify avarice, and extend corruption; to arrogate dominion without right, and practice cruelty without incentive." What does it say about our understanding of Johnson, that in the 225 years since his death, this thirty-page exposition of the origins of the slave trade has never appeared in any collected edition of Johnson's works? One hopes that the editors of the definitive Yale Edition of the Works of Johnson, begun in 1958 and still underway today, will decide to include it in a future volume.

A few months after the *World Displayed* appeared in mid-1759, slavery and racial issues surfaced in three different *Idler* essays. In the first, no. 81 (November 3, 1759), Johnson uses the monologue of a fictionalized American Indian to condemn the European conquest of America, in the course of which he inserts a protest against the slave trade: "When the sword and the mines have destroyed the natives, they [the Europeans] supply their place by human beings of another colour, brought from some distant country to perish here under toil and torture."[44] The following week, and surely not by chance, Johnson's friend Joshua Reynolds devoted part of his guest essay in *Idler* 82 to a discussion of how black people are as beautiful as whites because the aesthetics of human attraction are essentially subjective.[45] It seems likely that Reynolds, who would in the late 1780s support the abolitionist movement and who would paint more than one portrait of a black man during his career, shared Johnson's views and was prompted

---

43 "Introduction" to the *World Displayed*, printed in Alfred Hazen, ed., *Samuel Johnson's Prefaces and Dedications* (New Haven: Yale University Press, 1937), 227.

44 Samuel Johnson, *Idler* 81 (November 3, 1759), in *The Idler and The Adventurer*, in *The Yale Edition of the Works of Samuel Johnson*, ed. John M. Bullitt, W. J. Bate, and L. F. Powell, vol. 2 (New Haven: Yale University Press, 1963), 253.

45 *Idler* 82 (November 10, 1759), in *The Idler and The Adventurer*, 257, where Reynolds says: "It is custom alone determines our preference of the colour of the Europeans to the Aethiopians, and they, for the same reason, prefer their own colour to ours."

to write on this topic by Johnson's essay the week before, reinforcing Johnson's effort to show Native Americans and Africans as fully human and equal to Europeans.[46]

A month later, in an otherwise lighthearted *Idler* essay, the ugliness of slavery again pushes into Johnson's writing. Noting that earlier in history Europeans might never have believed in the existence of Africans "had only a single traveler related that many nations of the earth were black," Johnson concludes sardonically that by the mid-eighteenth century, thanks to the slave trade, such ignorance or denial is no longer possible because "of black men the numbers are too great who are now repining under English cruelty."[47] That same December, in reviewing John Hawkesworth's adaptation of Southerne's *Oroonoko* for the *Critical Review*, Johnson focused his six-page article on the most pointedly anti-slavery scenes and speeches that Hawkesworth had added to the play.[48] As Johnson produced these writings in 1759, Frank was somewhere at sea, his fate unknown, while Johnson fretted and wrote letters and pleaded with officials to find him and get him released from the navy. I suggest that we cannot continue to ignore the connections between Johnson's anxieties about Frank and the anti-slavery, anti-racism content of his writings during the same period.

There was one other major Johnson text of 1759 that, like Hawkesworth's *Oroonoko*, took as its hero an African prince: I refer of course to *Rasselas*. Written as his mother lay dying and he faced a life crisis, this powerful novella has been subjected to many kinds of psychological and biographical interpretation over the years. Imlac has been seen as representing Johnson himself, Imlac's foibles and utterances as Johnson's own, the mummies in the Egyptian catacombs as Johnson confronting his mother's imminent death, and so forth. Perhaps we can now add another biographical gloss. Are there not parallels between the young black man Rasselas, blessed with every protection and comfort, advised by his philosopher mentor to shun the dangers of the world and content himself with the safe domestic life he enjoys, nonetheless insisting on plunging

46   One of Reynolds's paintings, of a young black man, was long thought to be a portrait of Francis Barber himself, but scholars have recently questioned that attribution; see Michael Bundock, "From Slave to Heir: The Strange Journey of Francis Barber," *The New Rambler: Journal of the Johnson Society of London* Serial E VII (2003–2004): 23. Reynolds was one of six men who joined a dinner at Bennet Langton's London house in May 1787 to organize a legislative campaign against the slave trade and enlist Wilberforce to lead it. See Thomas Clarkson, *The History of the Rise, Progress, and Accomplishment of the Abolition of the African Slave-Trade by the British Parliament*, 2 vols. (London: Longman, Hurst, Rees, and Orme, 1808), 1:219–220 and 253.

47   *Idler* 87 (December 15, 1759), in *The Idler and The Adventurer*, 270.

48   *Critical Review* 7 (December 1759), 480–486. For details, see Basker, "Intimations of Abolitionism," 47–66.

out into the world to find himself, explore the world in all its variety, and necessarily subject himself to its difficulties and disasters, on the one hand, and, on the other, the young black man in Johnson's family who, despite his wise guardian's best efforts to guide and protect him, to provide education and comfort, nonetheless runs away from home to join the navy during wartime, sail the world in a battle ship, and drive his poor protector to distraction? Could young Rasselas not be, at least at the outset of the novel, a projection of the restless young Francis Barber, and might that not explain why the novel lingers so long in the Happy Valley, devoting the first fourteen chapters and some thirty percent of the text, to scenes of Rasselas chafing against confinement and pondering his own restlessness, before the action really begins? Could Frank's adolescent crisis have contributed to a crisis for Johnson himself, and helped prompt one of Johnson's richest meditations on the "hunger of the imagination" and the futility of trying to satisfy it with the occupations and gratifications of this world?

Frank's naval service marked a turning point in Johnson's life. Having been stirred into action on behalf of Frank over the two years he was away, Johnson began to take a more active role on behalf of black people in various contexts. In the spring of 1760, with Frank still at sea, Johnson made his first commitment to what might be called a black cause: he became a member of Dr. Bray's Associates. Originally founded in the 1730s, Dr. Thomas Bray's Associates was a Christian charity that in 1759 began redirecting its energies to founding and supporting schools for black children, both free and enslaved, in the British colonies. The Associates were elected members who donated their own money (a minimum of one guinea annually from each member), solicited from others, organized an annual sermon and dinner in London, hired and paid for missionary teachers abroad, sent books and other materials to the schools, and generally promoted an agenda of educating and Christianizing black children wherever schools could be organized. Nominated by Dr. John Burton of Eton and unanimously elected on March 6, 1760, Johnson was initiated at the meeting of May 1, 1760—a meeting at which he met and dined with Benjamin Franklin, himself recently elected and in the midst of helping to organize schools in Pennsylvania and other American colonies. Johnson remained a member of Bray's Associates for the rest of his life, donating every year, arranging for friends to join, such as George Strahan in the 1760s and Bennet Langton in the early 1780s, and at his death leaving them a legacy of cash and the rights to proceeds from his posthumously published *Prayers and Meditations*.[49] Other Johnson friends such as James Oglethorpe and the physician William Heberden, who attended Johnson on his deathbed, were also members. Although their official statements denied any intention of stirring up dissatisfaction or disobedience among slaves, their activities inevitably aroused the suspicions and resistance of slave owners, and placed Bray's Associates,

---

49   For details, see Maurice J. Quinlan, "Dr. Franklin Meets Dr. Johnson," *The Pennsylvania Magazine of History and Biography* 73 (1949): 42–43.

with their insistence that slaves were human, educable, and equal in God's eyes, in the position of proto-abolitionists in England and abroad.

Meanwhile, by the mid-1760s Johnson was allowing Frank to host gatherings of his black friends in his house, as witnessed by one startled visitor in 1765 who reported that when Frank opened the door, "a group of his African countrymen were sitting round a fire in the gloomy anti-room; and on their all turning their sooty faces at once to stare at me, they presented a curious spectacle."[50] More important than the visitor's casual racism is that at a time when in most of the British colonies gatherings of black people were suspect and forbidden by law, in London Johnson was opening his house to them. Were these gatherings purely social? Perhaps they had educational purposes? Were they organized to pursue literary or political discussion? Religious study? Literacy practice?

We may never know, but some light may be shed by the next of Johnson's decisive actions. In 1767, Johnson paid for Frank to enroll in a boarding school in Bishop's Stortford, where he was to continue studying for five years, until early 1772, at a total expense to Johnson of some 300 pounds. Despite the criticisms of Anna Williams and Sir John Hawkins, who saw it as a waste of money, most people have taken this, rightly, as a sign of Johnson's generosity toward Frank and faith in his ability to learn. How many men in the eighteenth century sent their servants—never mind *black* servants— to boarding school? But there is another question no one has asked. Why would Johnson send Frank away to school at the age of twenty-five and keep him there until age thirty? What purpose could attending a school that normally prepared teenage boys for university and the professions serve for Frank at his age? At this stage, we can only speculate, based on the little information we have. Perhaps in those sessions round the fire with his fellow black Londoners, Frank displayed a gift for teaching or for preaching, and Johnson thought to help Frank train for such a career? Or perhaps the model of the various overseas teachers hired by Bray's Associates to teach in the colonies inspired Johnson to envision Frank in that role? Or perhaps Johnson and Frank had been inspired by the example of Philip Quaque, a black African who had come to England from what is now Ghana in 1754, been educated and trained as a missionary, and then, with much fanfare in the press, been sent back to Cape Coast as a minister and teacher in 1766?[51] Whatever the reason that nothing came of Frank's boarding school education—did he fail to measure up? have a change of heart? fall in love?—Johnson showed no signs of disappointment. Instead, he continued to support and protect him with the ardor of a parent, as all the signs suggest, from the time in 1775 he closed a letter from Paris to housemate Robert Levet with the revealing phrase

50 Rev. Baptist Noel Turner, quoted in Reade, *Johnsonian Gleanings*, Part 2:15.

51 See *The Life and Letters of Philip Quaque, the First African Anglican Missionary*, ed. Vincent Carretta and Ty M. Reese (Athens: University of Georgia Press, 2010).

"Give my love to Francis," to the day a few years later when, to relieve their exigencies, he took Francis and his wife Elizabeth into his house to live with him.[52]

Isolated encounters show Johnson always treating black people with respect and humanity. In 1773 on the Scottish tour with Boswell, after traveling a day guided by Lord Monboddo's black servant Gory, Johnson was happy to see Gory getting along very amiably with Boswell's servant Joseph from Germany. "Those two fellows," said Johnson of the black and white servants riding together, "one from Africa, the other from Bohemia, seem quite at home." According to Boswell: "When Gory was about to part from us, Dr. Johnson called to him, 'Mr. Gory, give me leave to ask you a question! Are you baptized?' Gory told him he was,—and confirmed by the Bishop of Durham." Obviously pleased, Johnson "gave him a shilling."[53] In December 1780, when Ignatius Sancho died, leaving a widow and several children without support, Johnson offered to write the prefatory biography to a volume of Sancho's writings that was being gathered for publication by subscription, to raise funds for them. Sadly, Johnson never accomplished this task, which would have been the first biography of a black writer by a major English author in the history of literature. It was prevented only by another catastrophe, the sudden death in April of someone closer than family to him, his beloved friend and benefactor Henry Thrale.[54] Another episode from the 1770s shows how deeply Johnson empathized with and internalized the emotional suffering of those who had endured the slave trade. On March 25, 1776 he was having breakfast with Boswell at Lucy Porter's house in Lichfield. Suddenly a letter arrived announcing the death of the Thrales' only son, Harry, at the age of eleven. Johnson's sense of the devastating effect on the Thrales is conveyed in the metaphor that in the emotion of the moment he blurted out: "This is a total extinction of their family," he told Boswell, "as much as if they were sold into captivity."[55]

In the last decade of his life, Johnson attacked slavery in very public ways on at least two occasions. The first was in *Taxation No Tyranny* in 1775 which—despite its famous sound bite "How is it we hear the loudest *yelps* for liberty among the drivers of negroes?"—is more important for a proposal that Johnson endorsed elsewhere in the pamphlet: "It has been proposed," wrote Johnson, "that the slaves be set free, an act which surely the lovers of liberty cannot but commend. If they are furnished with the

---

52   Letter to Robert Levet, October 22, 1775, *Letters of Samuel Johnson*, 2:273.

53   *Boswell's Life*, 5:82–83.

54   *Letters of the Late Ignatius Sancho, An African*, Vincent Carretta, ed. (New York: Penguin, 1998), Introduction, ix and 248, note 1. See also Johnson to Joshua Reynolds, April 4, 1781, *Letters of Samuel Johnson*, 3:329: "Mr. Thrale died this morning."

55   *Boswell's Life*, 2:468–469.

arms for defence, and utensils for husbandry, and settled in some form of government within the country, they may be more grateful and honest than their masters."[56]

Americans and their sympathizers read this as a call for slave insurrections, and were horrified and outraged. Typical is the anonymous magazine writer who attacked Johnson for inciting rebellions that would "expose these devoted men [ie, the Americans] to the brutality of their own slaves." In July 1775, Benjamin Franklin wrote with indignation to a friend in London that Johnson's *Taxation No Tyranny* called for American slaves to rise up and "cut their Master's throats" and that he had heard "all the ministerial People recommended" Johnson's pamphlet, including Lord Dunmore, Royal Governor of Virginia, who had recently "taken some Steps towards carrying one part of [Johnson's] Project into Execution, by exciting an Insurrection among the Blacks."[57]

Even had Johnson been in a position to deny such accusations, it would have been pointless in the face of events. In November 1775 Lord Dunmore took matters a crucial step further, issuing a proclamation that offered freedom to American slaves who came over and fought on the British side. As many as 2,000 did, fighting as Dunmore's Ethiopian Regiment.[58] In July 1776 Thomas Jefferson included the incitement of insurrections among the grievances listed in his first draft of the Declaration of Independence. For the rest of the war British commanders encouraged and received runaway slaves into their ranks. Johnson had plunged himself into rancorous policy debates that seemed to many, including his former acquaintance and fellow Bray's Associate Benjamin Franklin, to have affected the course of the war in bloody ways, with reverberations for Americans and the slavery issue that would continue all the way down to John Brown's failed insurrection (1859) and Abraham Lincoln's Emancipation Proclamation (1863).

The second major occasion of Johnson's activism is the Joseph Knight trial, another story far too big and dramatic to be covered here. Two points about it will have to suffice. One is the eagerness with which Johnson involved himself, beginning the moment he heard about it from Boswell in June 1776. Johnson immediately wrote back to offer advice, to recommend precedents, and to donate money for legal expenses. "How is the suit carried on?" he asked Boswell, "If by subscription, I commission you to contribute, in my name, what is proper. Let nothing be wanting in such a case."[59]

56   Samuel Johnson, *Taxation No Tyranny*, in *Political Writings*, in *The Yale Edition of the Works of Samuel Johnson*, ed. Donald Greene, vol. 10 (New Haven and London: Yale University Press, 1977), 452. For detailed discussion of this pamphlet and American reaction, see Basker, "'The Next Insurrection': Johnson, Race, and Rebellion," 47–51.

57   Franklin to Jonathan Shipley, July 7, 1775, *The Papers of Benjamin Franklin*, ed. Leonard W. Laboree et al., 39 vols. (New Haven: Yale University Press, 1959–), 22:97.

58   Basker, "'The Next Insurrection': Johnson, Race, and Rebellion," 48–49.

59   To Boswell, July 2 and July 6, 1776, *Letters of Samuel Johnson*, 2: 348–350.

One can hear Johnson stressing that word *nothing*. By the end, Johnson would help edit Maclaurin's legal brief on behalf of Knight, compose and contribute his own anti-slavery legal argument for the case, and be invited by Lord Hailes, one of the justices who voted for Knight's freedom in January 1778, to edit the summary of the decision that Hailes was writing afterwards.[60] The most important point, finally, is the historic significance of the Joseph Knight decision: the case that Johnson so vigorously supported was to effectively abolish slavery in Scotland as of January 1778, making it the first country in Europe to achieve this distinction.[61]

One final piece of writing by Johnson may also qualify as part of his public campaign against slavery. That is his last will and testament, which, contrary to the advice of some, left the bulk of his estate, more than 1,500 pounds, to Francis Barber. Johnson's friend and biographer, the lawyer Sir John Hawkins, bitterly disapproved of Johnson's decision to leave his estate to Frank, criticizing it as "ostentatious bounty [and] favour to negroes."[62] Hawkins was on to something. He was concerned that Johnson's will—which was published and discussed in more than fifteen London newspapers within a week of his death[63]—appeared to be conscious display behavior, conveying a larger message to the public about the virtue of benefactions to former slaves. Much as George Washington would do fifteen years later when he freed his slaves in his will, Johnson was making a public statement through a private act. Johnson was suggesting, a bit like the reparationists today, that even when slavery had been abolished—which many people in the 1770s and 1780s mistakenly saw as a rapidly approaching inevitability—there was still much more that was due to its victims.[64]

I began this essay by saying I hoped to place Johnson in a new angle of vision, one that would help us to see him in a new way with regard to slavery and the history of race. I would like to close by giving the final word to one of Johnson's most intimate friends, someone who did see him at least partly in this light: Hester Thrale. Writing from Bath to a friend in London on December 7, 1789, just days before the fifth anniversary of Johnson's death, Hester Thrale Piozzi, as she was from 1784, relays all the news and gossip but devotes most of her letter to describing an extraordinary man who is the subject of all the attention and wonder in Bath:

60   *Boswell's Life*, 3:219.

61   In America, the state of Vermont prohibited slavery in its constitution when established in 1777. France would abolish slavery in 1794, but it would be reinstated by Napoleon in 1802 and persist until its final abolition in 1848.

62   Hawkins, *Life of Johnson*, 366.

63   See Helen Louise McGuffie, *Samuel Johnson and the British Press: A Chronological Checklist* (New York: Garland, 1976), 330–336.

64   Basker, "Johnson, Boswell, and the Abolition of Slavery," 43–44.

Bridge Tower the African Negro is that Subject, whose Son plays so enchantingly upon the Violin as to extort Applause from the first Professors—while his Father amazes me a hundred Times more by the showy Elegance of his Address—the polished Brilliancy of his Language, the Accumulation and Variety of his Knowledge, and the interesting Situation in which he stands towards an Absent Wife; who born a Polish Woman of high Rank in her own country, has been forcibly separated from him, who seems to run round the Globe with an Arrow in his Heart, and this astonishing Son by his Side.

She gushes that Bridgetower "would make a beautiful figure at the Bar of the House of Commons" and predicts that the poet Helen Maria Williams "will make such sweet verses about him when they meet."[65] She wishes that her friends might have a chance to meet Bridgetower, "to see what a Man may come to, tho' born a slave, and educated for no higher purpose" and she asks the rhetorical question that any thoughtful person of the time might have: "Was he sent hither by Providence to prove the Equality of Blacks to Whites?"

All her ruminations on Bridgetower come down, in the end, to a connection with Johnson. At the close of her letter, she offers this final observation on the impressive black man: "he is so very flashy a Talker, and has a Manner so distinguished for lofty Gayety, and universality of conversation I can but think all Day how Dr. Johnson would have adored that Man!"[66] The intensity of her sudden association of Bridgetower with Johnson is striking and powerful, and, given her closing exclamation point, I imagine her inner voice rising and stressing key words for dramatic emphasis: "I can but think *all Day* how Dr. Johnson would have *adored* that Man!" Like Hester Thrale Piozzi, I think we might do well to spend more of our days thinking about Johnson in connection with black people, their presence in his life and work, and in the collective consciousness of his time.

65   As Hester knew, Helen Maria Williams had already written in support of the anti-slavery movement: see her poem "On the Bill Which Was Passed in England for Regulating the Slave-Trade; A Short Time Before Its Abolition" (1788), in Basker, *Amazing Grace*, 371–372.

66   Hester Thrale Piozzi to Reverend Leonard Chappelow, December 7, 1789, *The Piozzi Letters*, ed. Edward A. Bloom and Lillian D. Bloom, 6 vols. (Newark: University of Delaware Press, 1989–2002), 1:330–331. Elsewhere, however, HTP recalled at least two occasions on which Johnson in conversation made negative comments about "negroes," even when defending Frank Barber: see Hester Lynch Piozzi, *Anecdotes of the Late Samuel Johnson, LL.D. During the Last Twenty Years of His Life* (London: T. Cadell, 1786), 153, 212–213.

Johnson on Blackmore, Pope, Shakespeare—and Johnson

James Engell

> Readers . . . are to impute to me whatever pleasure or weariness they
> may find in the perusal of Blackmore, Watts, Pomfret, and Yalden.[1]

This essay treats Johnson primarily through Sir Richard Blackmore, a novel path, and since many readers may not be acquainted with Blackmore's work, nor is there a compelling reason why anyone should be, I apologize at the outset. Yet, this path to Johnson provides understanding of his cherished personal values and of his deeply held principles of criticism. It reveals a central conflict holding in tension Johnson's personal life with his professional career.

I should like to present a piece of Johnson's writing that has, for 225 years, remained overlooked. On the surface, reasons appear for that. He wrote in 1780 about an author whose reputation had for decades been dark. While many of his *Lives of the Poets* are consulted more than the works of the poets they criticize, readers have found scant cause to consider his life of Blackmore. Short sections of one solitary article discuss its sources.[2] Scholars of Blackmore—Rosenberg, Solomon, Giacomini—quote the life, too.[3] It's a risky thing to speak of writing on which so few have commented even briefly, concerning an author whose poetry Johnson judged, in general, unmemorable, and whose prose he thought, on the whole, weak. Nonetheless, Johnson cared keenly about this life, and cared enough about some of Blackmore's work to make the effort to add it to the project when the booksellers had intentionally omitted Blackmore.

---

1 Samuel Johnson, "Watts," in *The Lives of the Poets*, in *The Yale Edition of the Works of Samuel Johnson*, ed. John H. Middendorf, vols. 21–23 (New Haven and London: Yale University Press, 2010), 23:1296 (hereafter cited as *Lives of the Poets*).

2 Pat Rogers, "Johnson's Lives of the Poets and the Biographical Dictionaries," *The Review of English Studies*, n.s. 31, no. 122 (1980): 149–171.

3 Albert Rosenberg, *Sir Richard Blackmore: A Poet and Physician of the Augustan Age* (Lincoln: University of Nebraska Press, 1953); Harry M. Solomon, *Sir Richard Blackmore* (Boston: Twayne, 1980); Michela Pizzol Giacomini, *Sir Richard Blackmore and the Bible: A Reading of His Physico-Theological Poems* (Lanham, Md.: University Press of America, 2007).

And why should we care? This life reveals, first, much about Johnson's attitude to Pope, Swift, and the wits surrounding them; second, something noteworthy about Johnson's religion and his habitual suspicion that religious, especially devotional, poetry must fall short of its subject; third, a good deal about Johnson's conceptions of ideal criticism; and, finally, this life discloses a fundamental tension running through the entire *Lives of the Poets*, a conflict in Johnson's professional *and* personal life, one that produces much of his best writing.

Johnson remarks that Blackmore's heroic poems "are now little read,"[4] and that "His works may be read a long time without the occurrence of a single line that stands prominent from the rest."[5] After the first edition, Johnson quotes not a single line of Blackmore's verse in the life proper. "Of his four epick poems the first had such reputation and popularity as enraged the criticks; the second was at least known enough to be ridiculed; the two last had neither friends nor enemies."[6] *Prince Arthur* (1695) was wildly received, *King Arthur* (1697) less so. *Eliza* (1705) attracted some notice, mostly negative, and *Alfred* (1723) was ignored.

Blackmore was also a prominent physician, yet of his medical books Johnson says, "By the transient glances which I have thrown upon them, I have observed an affected contempt of the ancients, and a supercilious derision of transmitted knowledge." (In terms of then contemporary medical knowledge, this now casts Blackmore in a favorable light.) Johnson speaks of Blackmore's "indecent arrogance" toward older learning and quotes one passage only to say it is "less reprehensible" than another he cites.[7] He states, "Blackmore's prose is not the prose of a poet; for it is languid, sluggish, and lifeless; his diction is neither daring nor exact, his flow neither rapid nor easy, and his periods neither smooth nor strong. His account of wit will shew with how little clearness he is content to think, and how little his thoughts are recommended by his language."[8]

At this point we might stop, as generations before have. Blackmore seems a prosaic poet, an arrogant physician, a failed critic. Isn't Johnson simply repeating the reasons Blackmore was already decanonized? Hadn't Dryden, Dennis, Pope, Swift, and others, at times goaded by political motives as well as by personal taste, succeeded in discrediting Blackmore? The coffin didn't need more nails, it was long in the ground. What were Johnson's motives? While he composed the life, Hester Thrale conjectured:

> That of Blackmore will be very entertaining, I dare say, and he will be rescued
> from the old wits who worried him, much to your disliking: so a little for love

4   *Lives of the Poets*, "Blackmore," 22:776n.

5   Ibid., 22:775.

6   Ibid., 22:771.

7   Ibid., 22:771–772.

8   Ibid., 22:766.

of his Christianity, a little for love of his physic, a little for love of his courage—and a little for love of contradiction, you will save him from his malevolent criticks, and perhaps do him the honour to devour him yourself—as a lion is said to take a great bull now and then from the wolves which had fallen upon him in the desert, and gravely eat him up for his own dinner.[9]

This gets closer to the mark. Johnson sent the life to her before publication and expressed anxiety about her judgment of it, intimating to her that she had disliked it (August 18, 1780). Two days later, sensing how important he thought the issue, she replied, "Blackmore's life is admirable; who says I don't like it?"[10]

However, the life did not turn out quite the lion's dinner she envisioned. There's more subtlety and discrimination, and something more deeply involved, than her image suggests. Regarding Johnson's aim in reviving Blackmore, let's examine the points mentioned earlier, some of which Hester Thrale has adumbrated.

First, let us look at Johnson's attitude to Pope and the "old wits" who "attacked" Blackmore.[11] He concludes that they made themselves enemies of Blackmore not from principles of critical objectivity but through envious, personal "malignity" aroused by the praise given Blackmore's first epic. Johnson also in part identifies with Blackmore, of whom he says, "his indigence compelled him to teach a school; an humiliation with which, though it certainly lasted but a little while, his enemies did not forget to reproach him, when he became conspicuous enough to excite malevolence; and let it be remembered for his honour, that to have been once a student-master is the only reproach which all the perspicacity of malice, animated by wit, has ever fixed upon his private life."[12] Johnson's memories of setting up as a schoolmaster himself at Edial, a choice of life that failed, remained with him, and throughout the *Lives* he says something about the teachers of poets. "Not to name the school or the masters of men illustrious for literature, is a kind of historical fraud, by which *honest* fame is injuriously diminished."[13]

Frequently, Johnson contrasts the "malice" and "malignity" of Pope and the other wits with the honest, even temper of Blackmore facing their vitriolic criticism. Blackmore was far the lesser poet, but as "the malignity of the wits," and "the animadversions of Dennis, insolent and contemptuous," as well as "tedious and disgusting,"[14] heaped derision on Blackmore, he responded without malice or personal attack, something

9 Letter to Samuel Johnson, May 9, 1780, Hester Lynch Piozzi, *Letters to and from the late Samuel Johnson. LL.D.* 2 vols. (Dublin: R. Montcrieffe et al., 1788), 2:122.

10 Ibid., 2:182.

11 *Lives of the Poets*, "Blackmore," 22:758.

12 Ibid., 22:755–756.

13 Ibid., "Addison," 22:598.

14 Ibid., "Blackmore," 22:759, 758.

unusual in those days of ad hominem criticism, unusual today as well. Dryden, too, "pursued him with great malignity," and the wits who in their "malice" courted Dryden's favor "easily confederated against" Blackmore.[15]

As the nastiness mounted, Blackmore rose above it. Johnson, altering a line from Pope himself, puts it this way: "of Blackmore it may be said, that as the poet sinks the man rises." When Blackmore wards off attacks of the wits, "he scorns to avert their malice at the expence of virtue or of truth."[16] Johnson implies that those two qualities were more cheaply valued at the wits' table. Johnson himself rarely responded to negative criticisms of his writing and let his own work, not a hot reply, speak for itself over time. Of Blackmore, Johnson says, "I hold him to have been very *honest*."[17]

By contrast, if we shift our eyes to Pope, we see that the most common word Johnson applies to Pope's life, character, and actions, as opposed to the genius of his poetry, is, repeatedly, "malignity": Pope's "tedious malignity"; "the incessant and unappeasable malignity of Pope"; "when Pope had exhausted all his malignity" on Cibber; or "his malignity to Philips."[18] Lyttelton, whom Johnson associates with Pope in political leanings, is characterized as "acrimonious and malignant."[19] Johnson refers to Swift's "long visit to Pope," and speaks of Swift, then "at fifty-nine the pupil of turpitude, and liable to the malignant influence of an ascendant mind." Further, "from the letters that pass between him and Pope it might be inferred that they, with Arbuthnot and Gay, had engrossed all the understanding and virtue of mankind . . ."[20]

Second, regarding Johnson's religion and his attitude to religious poetry, his treatment of Blackmore is revelatory. It isn't Blackmore's "Christianity," as Hester Thrale put it, that attracts Johnson. Many poets were Christians; Lyttelton became a devout Christian, yet Johnson's treatment of him and his work many considered unfair. Moreover, the religious poetry of Blackmore that Johnson praises is not explicitly Christian. Like the *Vanity of Human Wishes* it is theistic and pictures a fragile, desperate state of humankind unanchored by religious faith in God. Blackmore's poem *Redemption* (1722) Johnson mentions only to say that Blackmore wrote it because "he thought his undertaking imperfect, unless he likewise enforced the truth of revelation."[21] As far as poetry and religion are concerned, Johnson so often expressed doubts about the success or advisability of modern religious poetry that it would be difficult to cite all the instances, e.g., from "Waller," "Let no pious ear be offended if I advance, in

15   Ibid., 22:760, 767.

16   Ibid., 22:759, 767.

17   Ibid., 22: 760. Emphasis added.

18   Ibid., "Pope," 23:1145, 1152–1153, 1179.

19   Ibid., "Lyttelton," 23:1475.

20   Ibid., "Swift," 22:1019–1020.

21   Ibid., "Blackmore," 22:770.

opposition to many authorities, that poetical devotion cannot often please";[22] see also "Milton"[23] and "Denham."[24] About Watts, the great hymnist, he says, "his devotional poetry is, like that of others, unsatisfactory."[25]

So, it's unusual when Johnson recommends a religious poem with enthusiasm, and astonishing, given what he says about Blackmore's four epics on national subjects, that such a religious poem should be authored by Blackmore: *Creation, A Philosophical Poem* (1712) in seven books. Johnson thinks so well of it that he insists the booksellers print it entire in the collection, something they had planned to skip. This entailed cost and labor, for the poem runs about 4,800 lines! Physico-theological poetry was passing out of fashion late in the century, but Johnson warns, "Whoever judges of this by any other of Blackmore's performances, will do it injury";[26] it is by far his best. Dennis and Addison had lauded it, as did Cowper and Southey thereafter.

In *Creation* and nowhere else, Johnson states, Blackmore revised, sought aid, corrected, and re-corrected. As a result, Blackmore's *Creation*, "if he had written nothing else, would have transmitted him to posterity among the first favourites of the English Muse."[27] The revisions paid off handsomely, as such labor usually does, and they represent what Johnson would later call, referring to its greatest practitioner, who "excelled every other writer in it," "poetical prudence."[28] Johnson had originally underlined "poetical prudence" for emphasis. That excellent writer is Pope himself, who, malignant in criticism, Johnson sees as supremely gifted in the practice of poetry.

In paragraphs that conclude the life of Blackmore, Johnson again praises the versification, thought, diction, and design of *Creation*, its "varied excellence" and skillful blending of the didactic with the illustrative and descriptive. "To reason in verse is allowed to be difficult; but Blackmore not only reasons in verse, but very often reasons poetically."[29] Then, Johnson cannot resist jabbing sharply at Pope, not at his malignity but in this one case at his poetic inferiority to Blackmore: "This is a skill which Pope might have condescended to learn from him, when he needed it so much in his *Moral Essays*." (Pope's *Essay on Man*, especially the first epistle, owes very clear debts to *Creation*).[30] In this one instance, Blackmore's poetical prudence outstrips Pope's, and Johnson takes pains to point it out. Finally, to the literary merit of *Creation*, Johnson says must be added "the original position" of the poem, "the fundamental

22   Ibid., "Waller," 21:313–316.

23   Ibid., "Milton," 21:89.

24   Ibid., "Denham," 21:195.

25   Ibid., "Watts," 23:1306.

26   Ibid., "Blackmore," 22:762.

27   Ibid., 22:764.

28   Ibid., "Pope," 23:1185.

29   Ibid., "Blackmore," 22:775.

30   Solomon, *Sir Richard Blackmore*, 177–180.

principle of wisdom and of virtue."[31] Here, poetry and virtue go hand in hand. Today, we would likely read *Creation* as an anti-Lucretian poem promoting the idea of "intelligent design," yet we also need to recall that Blackmore wrote it well more than a century prior to the work of Charles Darwin, and that in Blackmore's time "intelligent design" was widely accepted as scientific.

Third, while Johnson's discussion of *Creation* has not gone unnoticed—scholars of Blackmore mention it—something else nearly has, and this is the fact that Johnson quotes at length from an essay Blackmore wrote for the periodical the *Lay-Monastery*, which appeared in late 1713. When Johnson first read it I've been unable to ascertain (he owned a copy of *Creation* while an undergraduate at Oxford),[32] but the passage he extracts from it is one of the longer quotations in the *Lives*, and one of the longest in prose from the direct subjects of Johnson's attention rather than from others who provide information about them. Johnson quotes from No. 2 (November 18, 1713).

This quotation is Blackmore's description of "a gentleman that owes to nature excellent faculties and an elevated genius, and to industry and application many acquired accomplishments."[33] Blackmore then provides the character of "a critic of the first rank; and, what is his peculiar ornament, he is delivered from the ostentation, malevolence, and supercilious temper, that so often blemish men of that character."[34] What follows reads like a mini-catalogue of key critical values and principles later invoked by Samuel Johnson: taste keen and practiced, spirited imagination but carefully considered ideas, knowledge of nature and the world, moral probity, judgment unswayed by previous authority merely for the sake of precedent, refusal to apply mechanically the rules of the ancients, the desire to produce something both useful and agreeable (what in the advertisement to the *Lives* is called "the honest desire of giving useful pleasure"), the willingness to praise as well as censure, a generous sense that no work can be perfect, the effort to be impartial, encouragement for the young, and an ability, occasionally, to write good poetry. Rarely have the principles of criticism espoused and practiced by Johnson himself been so clearly set out.

Johnson remarks that next to this critic the rest of the fraternity in the *Lay-Monastery* seem "but feeble mortals." He says little more about the entire passage, other than "there is no great genius in the design, nor skill in the delineation."[35] Why, then, does he quote it at length, especially when he could have selected from more than two dozen other papers by Blackmore, or quote none at all? He was drawn deeply to its critical ideals. He devotes far more space to them than he does, for example, to examining or quoting the qualities of the critic found in Pope's *Essay on Criticism*,

---

31   *Lives of the Poets*, "Blackmore," 22:776.

32   Aleyn Lyell Reade, *Johnsonian Gleanings*, 11 vols. (London: Francis & Company, 1909–1952), 5:227.

33   *Lives of the Poets*, "Blackmore," 22:764.

34   Ibid., 22:765.

35   Ibid., 22:764.

published the year before Blackmore's essay. If the paragraphs on criticism are argued to be mere paraphrases of Pope's *Essay on Criticism*, why doesn't Johnson indict Blackmore for that? He does attack Mallet for exactly such an operation.

When Johnson soon afterward writes his life of Pope, two remarks concerning his own approach to criticizing Pope's poetry directly echo the principles enunciated by Blackmore. "In him [Joseph Spence] Pope had the first experience of a critic without malevolence, who thought it as much his duty to display beauties as expose faults; who censured with respect, and praised with alacrity."[36] And, "the works of Pope are now to be distinctly examined, not so much with attention to slight faults or petty beauties, as to the general character and effect of each performance."[37] Fifteen years earlier, Johnson expressly characterized his own critical attitude to Shakespeare's qualities as a writer by declaring, "I shall show them . . . without envious malignity or superstitious veneration."[38]

The name of the critic Blackmore creates, "the hero of the club," the literary and intellectual gathering he heads, as Johnson's life points out, "is one Mr. Johnson."[39] This would have deepened the memory of it for Samuel Johnson and reinforced the identification he felt. When Johnson walked and rode with Garrick to London, he carried a letter of recommendation written by Gilbert Walmsley that asked the recipient, John Colson, to assist "one Mr. Johnson," who "is a very good scholar and poet . . ."[40] Johnson was amused and at times excited when he became mixed up with other Johnsons. As Sir John Hawkins noted, Johnson did not like being called *Dr.* Johnson; Boswell confessed that he rarely used that title, even in formal correspondence. After receiving the Oxford degree of Doctor of Civil Law, his second doctoral degree, he still called himself "Mr. Johnson."[41]

Samuel Johnson ends discussion of the passage by referring to Blackmore's critic as "the gigantick Johnson."[42] Perhaps a little skepticism and a lot of humor are at work here,

36   Ibid., "Pope," 23:1106.

37   Ibid., 23:1193.

38   Johnson's remarks are cited in *Johnson on Shakespeare*, in *The Yale Edition of the Works of Samuel Johnson*, ed. Arthur Sherbo, vols. 7–8 (New Haven and London: Yale University Press, 1968), 7: 71 (hereafter cited as *Johnson on Shakespeare*).

39   *Lives of the Poets*, "Blackmore," 22:764.

40   John Overholt and Thomas A. Horrocks, *A Monument More Durable Than Brass: The Donald & Mary Hyde Collection of Dr. Samuel Johnson* (Cambridge, Mass.: Houghton Library, 2009), 51–52.

41   Sir John Hawkins, *The Life of Samuel Johnson, LL.D.*, ed. O M Brack Jr. (Athens: University of Georgia Press, 2009), 268; *Boswell's Life of Johnson. Together with Boswell's Journal of a Tour to the Hebrides and Johnson's Diary of a Journey into North Wales*, ed. George Birkbeck Hill, rev. L. F. Powell, 6 vols. (Oxford: Clarendon Press, 1934–1950), 2:331–333, 332, n. 1.

42   *Lives of the Poets*, "Blackmore," 22:766.

but he also speaks of "all his abilities" and his "constellation of excellence."[43] This may be mixed with Johnson's awareness of his own now huge reputation and the phrases (for example, "Great Cham" or "Ursa Major," which itself names a constellation) used to describe his own person and powers. As far as I can tell, only Larry Lipking, in his 1998 book *Samuel Johnson: The Life of an Author*, has drawn any attention to "gigantick Johnson" and Samuel Johnson's sense of an ideal critic.[44] Roger Lonsdale calls the Johnson-Johnson connection "self-mocking" and a "joke," yet, citing only Lipking, remarks what small attention it has received.[45] It is self-mocking perhaps, but with a serious side, too.

Fourth, Johnson contrasts Blackmore's lack of genius—accompanied by his virtue, piety, and good will—with the consummate genius, the supreme "poetical prudence" of Pope, who expended against Blackmore all that young envy and later mature malignity, prompted by his own sense of superiority, could muster.

This uncovers the central tension in the *Lives*, one that creates not only unease and conflict but also profound insight throughout Johnson's life and work: the exceptional literary genius or wit may not be the good person at all, and the good person often lacks genius, or even talent, while hoping for it. We see this tension even in little remarks; for example, Johnson says of Pope, "He passed over peers and statesmen to inscribe his Iliad to Congreve, with a magnanimity of which the praise had been compleat, had his friend's virtue been equal to his wit."[46]

Why did Blackmore so often fall short if he could, according to Johnson, soar high in *Creation*? Because in his other poems, "Having formed a magnificent design, he was careless of particular and subordinate elegancies; he studied no niceties of versification; he waited for no felicities of fancy; but caught his first thoughts in the first words in which they were presented; nor does it appear that he saw beyond his own performances, or had ever elevated his views to that ideal perfection which every genius born to excel is condemned always to pursue, and never overtake."[47] Perhaps recalling this passage, Coleridge, too, conceives qualities of the poet in "*ideal* perfection."[48] What for Johnson sets apart "genius born to excel" from mediocrity is sheer intellect coupled with obsessive craft; it has little to do with personal virtue. This attitude calls

43   Ibid., 22:766, 764.

44   Lawrence Lipking, *Samuel Johnson: The Life of an Author* (Cambridge, Mass.: Harvard University Press, 1998), 272–273.

45   Samuel Johnson, *The Lives of the Most Eminent English Poets; With Critical Observations on their Works*, ed. Roger Lonsdale, 4 vols. (Oxford: Clarendon Press, 2006), 3:331, n. 27 (hereafter cited as *Lives of the Most Eminent English Poets*).

46   *Lives of the Poets*, "Pope," 23:1172.

47   Ibid., "Blackmore," 22:775.

48   Samuel Taylor Coleridge, *Biographia Literaria or, Biographical Sketches of My Literary Life and Opinions*, ed. James Engell and W. Jackson Bate, 2 vols. (Princeton: Princeton University Press, 1983), 2:14.

to mind the sentiment later attributed to Valéry, that no poem is ever finished but only abandoned in despair.[49] Likewise, Theodor Adorno remarks, "No improvement is too small or trivial to be worthwhile. Of a hundred alterations each may seem trifling or pedantic by itself; together they can raise the text to a new level."[50]

It's easy now to pass over the fact that what Johnson is saying is a matter of major importance in the annals of criticism. Again, Blackmore's purpose in writing was, according to Johnson, nobler than Pope's, for it was "not for a livelihood" but "if he may tell his own motives . . . to engage poetry in the cause of virtue."[51] Indeed, he provoked "the unremitted enmity of the wits . . . *more* by his virtue than his dullness."[52] Still, Blackmore remains a markedly inferior poet. At a time later in the century when Joseph Warton and others were demoting Pope as incapable of sublimity, passion, or pure poetry, Johnson goes out of his way to defend Pope's genius and to argue for Pope's place in the first rank. The chiasmus of Blackmore's poetic mediocrity yet sterling character crossing Pope's "poetical prudence" and "genius" yet "incessant malignity" means that, once and for all, the *Lives* destroy any comforting convictions that a great writer must in any way be a good or even decent person, and they confirm that a most admirable individual may desperately aspire to artistic distinction and never, despite early fame, reach even its lower rungs. For Blackmore, *Creation* is the exception that proves the rule.

We may congratulate ourselves for taking this for granted today, almost as child's play, but for many of Johnson's audience, and in a critical tradition moving from at least as early as Quintilian, down through Ben Jonson, and permeating many neo-classical critics, virtue and poetry seemed inseparable. Running against this grain, Johnson deliberately identifies Shakespeare's chief fault this way: "he sacrifices virtue to convenience," a judgment that shocks some readers even today, especially when we add to it his claim that Shakespeare's faults "are sufficient to obscure and overwhelm any other merit."[53] Even the highest genius misses an ethical beat and, according to Johnson, misses it often. Without overt statement but in the *Lives* by massive evidence and critical acuity, Johnson rejects the theory that only a good person can be a good poet and a good poet must perforce be a good person. This tenet becomes untenable. The genius of the wits exceeds that of Blackmore by as much or more as their malignity outdistances his virtue. Yet for Johnson the good *critic* should be objective, free from

---

49   Paul Valéry, "Au Sujet du 'Cimetière Marin,'" in *Variété III* (Paris: Gallimard, 1936), 56; Ralph Keyes, *The Quote Verifier: Who Said What, Where, and When* (New York: St. Martin's Press, 2006), 167.

50   Theodor W. Adorno, *Minima Moralia: Reflections from a Damaged Life*, trans. E. F. N. Jephcott (London: Verso, 1978), sec. 51: 85.

51   *Lives of the Poets*, "Blackmore," 22:757.

52   Ibid., 22:773–774, emphasis added.

53   *Johnson on Shakespeare*, 7:71.

professional enmity, malignity, personal envy, and scores to settle. In this sense, the good critic must be virtuous.

The nub of the matter as far as Blackmore is concerned, is, as Johnson says, "that malignity takes hold only of his writings, and that his life passed without reproach."[54] The *Lives of the Poets* themselves, as a collected body, take up the character and manners of writers in public conduct and private life as well as the quality of their productions. On April 2, 1779, Johnson notes in his *Diary*: "Last week I published the lives of the poets written I hope in such a manner, as may tend to the promotion of Piety."[55] By *honesty* of observation, perhaps as much as is granted to any one individual, Johnson provides the first massive work of criticism that draws both one line clearly separating, and another line suggestively connecting, the content of character in real life and the content of art. The line drawn to connect life and work may already be illustrated by the motive he ascribes to Shakespeare's fault of sacrificing virtue to convenience: "His first defect is that to which may be imputed most of the evil in books *or* in men."[56] After all, Johnson had devoted several *Rambler* essays to the difference between an author's life and work.

The *Lives* represent the first time that any critic had, clearly, convincingly, and elaborately, drawn the connections *and* the boundaries between lived experience and literary excellence, between virtue and genius, on such a scale, for such a significant part of an artistic tradition, in the entirety of western art. What made this possible? The increasing availability of biographical information, Johnson's own intimate, often personal acquaintance with many of the poets and their circles, his candor, his unrivalled knowledge of the minute qualities of their work not only in themselves but compared with a much larger body of literature in several languages ancient and modern, his sympathy, and his virtue—in short, the qualities of "gigantick Johnson." Criticism would not again be the same, nor would literary biography. Frequently a close though rarely a sympathetic reader of Johnson's criticism, Coleridge would nevertheless express the matter similarly: "In other works," such as poetry, "the communication of pleasure may be the immediate purpose; and though truth, either moral or intellectual, ought to be the *ultimate* end, yet this will distinguish the character of the author, not the class to which the work belongs."[57]

Was Johnson satisfied with the frequent rift between personal virtue and poetic genius? He wished it away but knew his wish futile. He so felt the neglect and malice heaped on Blackmore that he added that life to his labor for no additional payment. He wished to rescue Blackmore and diligently sought materials for that life, while he once

---

54 *Lives of the Poets*, "Blackmore," 22:774.

55 Samuel Johnson, *Diaries, Prayers, and Annals*, in *The Yale Edition of the Works of Samuel Johnson*, ed. Donald and Mary Hyde, vol. 1 (New Haven and London: Yale University Press, 1958), 294.

56 *Johnson on Shakespeare*, 7:71. Emphasis added.

57 Coleridge, *Biographia Literaria*, 2:12.

declined information about Swift from Swift's relative,[58] and testily rejected information about Pope, too, though later recanted and valued it. Even though Swift and Pope fall in the late-middle of the chronology determined by the booksellers, the three writers Johnson most closely links in "malignity," "malevolence," and "malice," Pope, Swift, and Lyttelton, are precisely the last three whose lives he composes, with Pope's the very last. This does not prove cause and effect but suggests it. To their malignity Johnson contrasts "the honours" of Blackmore's "magnanimity," not only as a person but even "as an author."[59] This is a great, productive tension in Johnson: he devoted himself to a profession, undertaking, and practice, that of literature, in which those who excel in genius and accomplishment often fall short of or contradict flatly the inner moral life of virtue to which Johnson devoted himself not equally but even more.

Commenting on certain lines in Gray's ode *The Progress of Poesy* (1757), Johnson criticizes the reality represented by the lines, yet concludes, "But that poetry and virtue go always together is an opinion so pleasing, that I can forgive him who resolves to think it true."[60] He doesn't say "an *illusion* so pleasing," nor does he say he "can forgive him who *is misled* to think it true." He sympathizes with the ideal but knows in reality that it is not always, perhaps not often, true. He believes that one of his motives as a critic to undertake the *Lives* is "the promotion of Piety," meaning not religion narrowly understood, but the large sense of virtuous conduct running through privacy, family, faith, community, country, and humanity. The moral life is here, though in a critic we may occasionally resist it. But that criticism and virtue go always together is an opinion so pleasing, that perhaps we can forgive whoever resolves to make it true.

58   *Lives of the Most Eminent English Poets*, 4:428.
59   *Lives of the Poets*, "Blackmore," 22:774.
60   Ibid., "Gray," 23:1466.

Vindicating Milton: Poetic Misprision in Johnson's *Dictionary of the English Language*

Allen Reddick

HE RICH REPOSITORY OF TEXT(S) TO BE FOUND IN Samuel Johnson's great *Dictionary of the English Language* (1755) presents an array of evidence, evidence potentially relevant to investigations of the structure of historical and linguistic, cultural and ideological phenomena. It also contains material relating to Samuel Johnson's intentions and procedures, and his attitudes to culture, politics, letters, and language, and to the inherited writings of his ancestors. The nature of this evidence is complex, however, because of the particular type of text the *Dictionary* manifests. Approaching this complexity requires a careful sensitivity to the life of text, context, and intertextuality. What constitutes evidence in the *Dictionary*, and evidence of or for what? How should the evidence be treated? Johnson's *Dictionary* was the first dictionary in English to include illustrations from authors to act as "authorities" and examples for the definitions and notes on usage; these tens of thousands of quotations have presented particular opportunities and challenges for scholars. Johnson's innovation provides a remarkable resource for investigations into his *Dictionary*, his attitudes, and literary history more generally. For some time, however, I have advised caution in the interpretation of the illustrative quotations, while still attempting to explore fruitful opportunities.[1]

Occasionally, scholars make the mistake of assuming that authors quoted in the *Dictionary* are to be taken in their unmediated voice—quoting themselves, as it were, making statements or proclamations, in a kind of collaboration with Johnson. Another invalid assumption is that the quoted authorities necessarily voice Johnsonian views. Similarly, to claim to know what "Johnson says" in the work, whether in relation to the *Dictionary*'s quotations or to the work as a whole, is not entirely coherent. Asserting "what the *Dictionary* says . . .," or "the position adopted by the *Dictionary* is . . ." is equally problematic. The *Dictionary* does not provide the kind of coherence or unity of

---

1 For example, *The Making of Johnson's Dictionary, 1746–1755*, 2nd rev. ed. (Cambridge: Cambridge University Press, 1996); "Johnson Beyond Jacobitism: Signs of Polemic in the *Dictionary* and the Life of Milton," *English Literary History* 64 (1997): 983–1005; and "Johnson's *Dictionary of the English Language* and Its Texts: Quotation, Context, Anti-Thematics," *Yearbook of English Studies* 28 (1998): 66–76. Portions of this essay have been adapted from my article, "Past and Present in Samuel Johnson's *Dictionary of the English Language*," *International Journal of Lexicography* 23 (2010): 207–222.

text-type (narrative, rhetorical, argumentative, educational, etc.) that we would expect with other kinds of texts, even if that perceived coherence is often illusory. Yet the temptations are always there to fall into easy patterns of taking the text—specifically the authorities—at face value, which leads to a variety of fallacies concerning voice and agency.

Johnson originally wished to add quotations to his *Dictionary* that would go beyond a simple exemplifying function, so that "every quotation should be useful to some other end than the illustration of a word." Yet he made clear in his Preface that this was seldom possible. "The examples, thus mutilated, are no longer to be considered as conveying the sentiments or doctrine of their authours." Many of his quotations, he admits in the Preface, "serve no other purpose, than that of proving the bare existence of words."[2] The first purpose for which Johnson quotes a passage is exemplification of the given sense under a word heading. Beyond this, the voice and the extent of the declamation of the quoted author and passage, as well as the citation itself, are equivocal, more or less eloquent depending on Johnson's arrangement of the entry and the general rhetoric allowed or encouraged under the heading or sub-heading. The quotations are concerned primarily with a fairly restricted lexical function. And they are decontextualized, obviously, from their original contexts.[3]

In examining the evidence provided by the incorporated quotations, it is necessary to take into consideration a variety of factors, of which the following are just a few. Importantly, we must consider context, both prior and current. We must note the extent and kind of attribution Johnson provides, which reveal the ways in which the source authority is being invoked. The extent and kind of reference to a particular author or work may have implicit connotations, as well. The placement of the quotation in relation to the other elements of the entry, and to some extent the other entries on the page, may be relevant to an assessment of its significance, in particular the relation of quotation to definition. (It should be kept in mind that for the most part, Johnson and his amanuenses first selected the quotations, which in turn generated the definitions and other parts of the entry, as glosses on the word as quoted.) Ideally, we should even consider the location of the passage in the physical source from which it was taken by Johnson or his amanuensis and how it may have been marked and copied out, in order to determine the extent of Johnson's responsibility and/or intention for the quotation's presence, form, and attribution in the completed entry.[4]

Freya Johnston's insightful essay, "Accumulation in Johnson's Dictionary," illustrates the mistakes one can make, on the one hand, and the insights into Johnson's thinking

2   Samuel Johnson, Preface to the *Dictionary*, in *Johnson on the English Language*, in *The Yale Edition of the Works of Samuel Johnson*, ed. Gwin J. Kolb and Robert De Maria Jr., vol. 18 (New Haven: Yale University Press, 2005), 93, 94, 94–95 (hereafter cited as *Johnson on the English Language*).

3   Reddick, "Johnson's *Dictionary of the English Language* and Its Texts," 66–76.

4   See especially ibid.

and instincts the material makes possible, on the other. She writes that Johnson's quotations under CHILD demonstrate that in the *Dictionary* "the mention of children leads to thoughts of death" because the sources are quoted from contexts related to the death of children.[5] Yet the quotations have been completely de-contextualized each from its own source, then re-contextualized, and make no reference whatsoever to children and death—in fact, they read, for the most part, rather promisingly in their new context concerning relations between parents, children, and fruitfulness. Regardless of previous context, how do the quotations function in the new context? Johnston does not address this question. Yet while her comment has no bearing on the *Dictionary* itself, she succeeds in uncovering a pattern in the selection of passages, illuminating important possibilities for Johnson's reading, train of thought, and preoccupations, particularly displayed in his searches for illustrations. Indeed, all the original contexts do concern the death of children.

In this spirit we can consider the ways in which some of Johnson's quoting and intertextualizing of material is relevant to his attitudes and intentions, including his intentions in the *Dictionary*. I wish to look at Johnson's treatment of Milton's poetry and the ways in which he quotes, misquotes, alters, bends, or breaks his material. Such "misprision" suggests not only Johnson's intentions for the *Dictionary* and Milton's place within it, but also Johnson's attitudes towards Milton more generally, his poetry, and place in literary as well as political history.

In the revised fourth edition of the *Dictionary* (1773) and the "Life of Milton" (1779), as well as the political pamphlets of the 1770s, Johnson aggressively repositions Milton within literary, sacred, and political history. In the *Dictionary*, he almost completely omits Milton's prose, the major source of his politics, and in the "Life," he denigrates Milton's prose writings as self-interested and perverse. Yet he floods the fourth edition with new quotations from *Paradise Lost*. Under the adjective GREAT, for example, he adds no fewer than nineteen new quotations from *Paradise Lost*. The "Life of Milton" praises the poem as the greatest ever written in English. This is part of an attempt to rearrange Milton's political capital and salvage and enhance his sacred worth. It is an effort of "re-placement" from historical Milton as republican and dangerous, into the timeless, as the greatest sacred poet. As for the political pamphlets, he engages in a battle (with the likes of John Adams and others) for the meaning and use of Milton for political and cultural propagandistic purposes.[6]

---

5   Freya Johnston, "Accumulation in Johnson's *Dictionary*," *Essays in Criticism* 57 (2007): 314.

6   See Reddick, "Johnson Beyond Jacobitism," 983–1005; Bruce Redford, "Defying our Master: The Appropriation of Milton in Johnson's Political Tracts," *Studies in Eighteenth-Century Culture* 20 (1990): 81–92, and for Johnson and Adams, see Reddick, "Introduction" to William H. Bond, "'From the Great Desire of Promoting Learning': Thomas Hollis's Gifts to the Harvard College Library," *Harvard Library Bulletin* 19, nos. 1–2 (2008): 17–18.

Two examples are obvious digs at Milton—the writer and the ideas he articulated in his prose, as well as his physical person and stature. The entry for SONNET reads as follows: "1. A short poem consisting of fourteen lines, of which the rhymes are adjusted by a particular rule. It is not very suitable to the English language, and has not been used by any man of eminence since *Milton*." Johnson then proceeds to quote the entire text of Milton's "Sonnet XI" ("A book was writ of late called Tetrachordon"), as if to display the unsuitableness of the form for English. Milton's poem was written in response to his divorce tracts being largely ignored and unappreciated. Johnson had already written in the "Life" that "There seems not to have been much written against him [i.e., his divorce tracts], nor any thing by any writer of eminence. . . . He complains of this neglect in two sonnets, of which the first ["Sonnet XI"] is contemptible, and the second [*XII*] not excellent." As Roger Lonsdale points out, William Hayley, in his *Life of Milton* of 1796, "suggested that SJ did so to show M's poetry at its worst."[7] Hayley was certainly correct. Not only does Johnson require it to function as an example of poor poetry and misspent effort, but he also proceeds to display the unsuitableness of the form for English. Quoted in its entirety, the sonnet is completely out of proportion to the rest of the entry and to the *Dictionary* pages themselves: it is the longest passage of poetry quoted under the entries from "S," and possibly the longest in the entire *Dictionary*. The poem is rather rough, arrogant, and satirical, presumably mocking the uneducated rabble with whom he must contend. It includes pseudo-rustic phrasing and semi-comic rhymes like these: "now seldom pord on:/ . . . Bless us, what a word on/A title-page is this!" (ll. 4–6), and "some in file/ . . . might walk to Mile-/End-green"(ll. 6–8). The quotation displays Milton's poetic talents in a poor light, implies his snobbish and sour attitude towards the people, and reflects negatively on his ambitions for the divorce tracts. By drawing attention to itself, the sonnet becomes ludicrously bathetic. There could also be a joke on Milton's poetry always seeming to be longer than anyone else's—in this case, even his unappealing sonnet dwarfs all others. (Johnson would quote lines 9–12 from "Sonnet XII," "I did but prompt the age to quit their clogs," in the epigraph to *The Patriot*, as an ironic appropriation of Milton's protest.)

Revising the entry LATTERLY, adv., for the fourth edition of 1773, Johnson adds the following quotation, the sole illustration under this entry: "*Latterly* Milton was short and thick. *Richardson*." In his favorable biography of Milton (1734), Jonathan Richardson had actually written: "He was rather a Middle Siz'd than a Little Man, and Well Proportion'd; Latterly he was—No; Not short and Thick, but he would have been So, had he been Somthing [*sic*] Shorter and Thicker than he Was."[8] Johnson had

7   Johnson, *The Lives of the Most Eminent English Poets; with Critical Observations on Their Works, With Introduction and Notes by Roger Lonsdale*, 4 vols. (Oxford: Clarendon Press, 2006), 1:252, 384; William Hayley, *Life of Milton*, 2nd ed. (London: T. Cadell, 1796), xii, note.

8   *The Early Lives of Milton*, Helen Darbishire, ed. (London: Constable, 1932), 201; I was first alerted to these references by Christine Rees in her lecture at the Pembroke College, Oxford, conference, "Johnson at 300," September 2009. See her *Johnson's Milton* (Cambridge: Cambridge University Press, 2010), 236–237.

already uncharitably noted Milton's apparently unattractive stature in his "Life of Milton": having described his hair as "according to the picture which he has given of Adam," Johnson continues, "He was, however, not of the heroick stature, but rather below the middle size, according to Mr. Richardson, who mentions him as having narrowly escaped from being *short and thick*."[9] Needless to say, Johnson knows what Richardson actually said, but turns it, in the "Life," into a bathetic diminution of the "great man," who was in fact not "great." By using the words "having narrowly escaped from," Johnson substitutes a battle with the waistline, or at any rate with his figure, for his reputed heroic struggles.

Most of Johnson's individual instances of quoting Milton in the *Dictionary* seem to be innocuous or un-ideological, although there are quite a few cases which might appear to be self-reflexive, especially in consideration of Milton's biography and his symbolic capital—these are contexts dealing with the subversion of authority, war between heaven and hell, betrayal, etc., all potential themes that could recoil upon the author Milton, especially in the hands of the politically unfriendly Johnson. Some of these quotations may or may not be intentionally ironic. In a few cases, Johnson uses Milton in the *Dictionary* for mock-heroic effect, the effect mocking Milton himself. We see this with examples of SONNET and LATTERLY which also have a mock-heroic quality. Some of these instances are highlighted, for the scholar at least, and any interested contemporary, because they are added in the fourth edition of 1773. Each is placed under potentially sensitive political words.

To illustrate the definition, "Opponent to lawful authority," under REBELLIOUS, Johnson adds the following passage from the description of Satan in Book III of *Paradise Lost*:

> Bent he seems
> On desperate revenge, which shall redound
> Upon his own *rebellious* head.
> *Milton.*

Upon Milton's own "*rebellious* head" Johnson exacts a type of revenge, aligning him with positions or suggestions he would in fact have opposed as Cromwell's Latin Secretary and the apologist for the execution of Charles I. Johnson characteristically reduces Milton's historical and political stature while invoking his poetic stature. This constitutes a version of what Bruce Redford, in discussing Johnson's treatment of Milton in the pamphlet *The Patriot*, identifies Johnson to be undertaking, "To align himself with Milton, yet repudiate him at the same time."[10] He both diminishes him

---

9   *Lives of the Poets*, 1:273–274.

10   Redford, "Defying our Master," 88.

and recruits him as an authority. Johnson uses Milton's authority, and it appears that Milton must bend under the example of Satan to demonstrate appropriate obeisance.

Consider the 1773 fourth-edition revisions Johnson makes to his first-edition text for the entry PARDON n.s. Under the definition, "Forgiveness of a crime; indulgence," Johnson adds three quotations, each from *Paradise Lost*. Within such a sensitive entry in relation to Milton's biography, they appear to me significant in reading Johnson's attitude towards Milton: the first two thus are explicit and intended self-references; the third indicates Johnson's attitude towards and reading of Milton. By dropping the semantic extension, "indulgence," Johnson places the focus on "forgiveness" and "crime." The first passage, from *Paradise Lost*, bk. 11, line 167, Eve's "But infinite in *pardon* is my judge," is altered into the present tense from the poem's original "was." The second quotation is taken from Adam's directions to Eve in *Paradise Lost*, bk 10, lines, 1086–1090:

> What better can we do than prostrate fall
> Before him reverent, and there confess
> Humbly our faults, and *pardon* beg, with tears
> Wat'ring the ground?

Johnson's ironic quoting of the lines from Eve/Adam/Milton under such a delicate entry as PARDON co-opts Milton's voice in such a way that it serves as a self-reference, and self-censorship, of Milton's own transgression, forced humility, and repentance, before his own merciful judge, Charles II, God's earthly regent. The original passage in the poem contains the spatial reference "What better can we do than to the place/ Repairing where he judged us, prostrate fall" (X, 1086–1087), which is deleted in the quotation, thus translating the site of the action to Milton's own situation. The lack of antecedent for "we" perhaps implicates Milton and the whole band of republican leaders and apologists. The passage as quoted seems an echo of the conclusion of Dryden's *Absalom and Achitophel* in which the monarch Charles II, God the Father, and we the reader judge—and nod affirmatively—in perfect agreement. We can contrast this example with Johnson's quoting of lines 1088–1092, which he added in the fourth edition. These illustrate MEEK adj. 2, in which the passage is adapted to refer to "Both," i.e., Adam and Eve, ("Both confess'd/Humbly their faults . . .") and by alteration of the tense is placed in the past tense, thus clearly referring to the sacred story. In this case, there is no noticeable ironic or rhetorical use of Milton's lines. The passage was one Johnson was eager to incorporate into the *Dictionary*.

The third quotation he adds would sound more like Pope's *Dunciad* than Milton's *Paradise Lost*, were it in heroic couplets:

> There might you see
> Indulgencies, dispenses, *pardons*, bulls,
> The sport of Winds.

The passage is in fact abridged from *Paradise Lost*, bk. 3, lines 489–493, in which Milton describes "the Limbo of Vanity," a comical description of religious abuses and their practitioners in the Catholic church:

> Then might ye see
> Cowls, hoods, and habits, with their wearers, tost
> And fluttered into rags; then reliques, beads,
> Indulgences, dispenses, pardons, bulls,
> The sport of winds.

This passage is an imitation, or adaptation, of Ariosto's *Orlando furioso*, canto XXXIV, stanzas 73ff., the episode of the limbo of vanity on the moon. In the mock-epic catalog of detritus as "sport of winds," Milton seems to imitate Pope, rather than the other way around; the presentation of the mock-epic Milton, in lines Johnson elsewhere deprecated, diminishes Milton to the familiar and coarse. Johnson's quoting of half-lines disguises the blank-verse-epic lines, blurring boundaries between possible poetic modes. Milton not only appears to be imitating Pope, or a lesser mock-epic poet like Garth, rather than the true epic poet, Ariosto; as Johnson had written of *Paradise Lost* in his "Life of Milton," "[Milton's] desire of imitating Ariosto's levity has disgraced his work [*Paradise Lost*] with the *Paradise of Fools*; a fiction . . . too ludicrous for its place." Critics including Dryden, Addison, and Voltaire had objected to this episode in *Orlando furioso*.[11] Johnson quotes this passage under three different entries: he quotes this passage slightly differently under DISPENSE n.s., and quotes the lines immediately following this passage under LIMBO n.s., def. 1, in the first and fourth editions. In so doing, he reduces Milton in stature, subtly reminding readers that Milton's sarcasm and arrogance rendered him ridiculous. In the progress of the entry, Milton not only repents and seeks pardon (in the first quotation), he is tamed into the mock-heroic, the heir of Dryden and Pope.

Johnson often quotes, in the *Dictionary* and elsewhere, the following passage:

> I may assert eternal providence,
> And *vindicate* the ways of God to man.
> > > *Milton.*

---

11   *Lives of the Poets*, 1:292, 430.

This passage illustrates definition 4 of the verb, To VINDICATE, for example, in his *Dictionary*. The lines were obviously important to him, as he inserts them (in 1773) to illustrate GREAT (with "men" for "man"), he quotes it earlier in his *Rambler* 94 on Milton's prosody, and again in his "Life of Milton" in 1779. While the passage sounds familiar—and who does not recognize the most famous line in *Paradise Lost?*—the line is not Milton's. Instead, it is Pope's, from the *Essay on Man* (1733–1734), yoked by violence to Milton's invocation, above Milton's own name. Milton's poem reads, seemingly unforgettably, "I may assert eternal providence,/And *justify* the ways of God to men" (bk. 1, lines 25–26). How could it have come to this? Johnson is substituting a line from a poem he famously did not care for (the *Essay on Man*), whose theology he distrusted, for Milton's line, the very line, in Johnson's words in his *Life of Milton*, which delineated the "purpose . . . the most useful and the most arduous" in poetry, "to shew the reasonableness of religion, and the necessity of obedience to the Divine Law."[12]

It might be insisted that the difference between "vindicating" and "justifying" is not great—indeed, Johnson defines the verbs similarly and in part reciprocally in the *Dictionary*. In the 1749 edition Johnson used, however, Milton's editor Thomas Newton, for one, found no equivalence between the terms and criticized Pope's variation as petty: "It is not easy to conceive any good reason for Mr. Pope's preferring the word *vindicate*, but Milton makes use of the word *justify*, as it is the Scripture word, *That thou mightest be justified in thy sayings, Rom.* III. 4. And *the ways of God to Men* are justified in the many argumentative discourses throughout the poem, and particularly in the conferences between God the Father and the Son."[13] Milton himself puns on the senses of "justify," alluding to Protestant justification by faith. Reading it as "vindicate" alters the theology of the line: Johnson's mistake—if we assume that it is one—is hardly neutral. He incorporates Pope's cleansing of the line of its Protestant insistence. If Johnson were not the great critic of Milton, it would seem a mere curiosity.

In the realms of religion and moral philosophy, Johnson would probably in many ways have sided more with Milton than with Pope. The opening to Pope's poem and the entire poem itself omit all references to revealed religion, to Christ, and to the hereafter. Pope invites comparison with Milton's breathtaking declaration of theme and intention—his claims to defend and amplify God's entire prophetic narrative scheme. Yet Pope's opening lines meander like the maze he originally described as "without a plan." He changed that to "but not without a plan," yet the section remains decidedly this-worldly:

> Let us (since Life can little more supply
> Than just to look about us and to die)

---

12   *Lives of the Poets*, 4:76–77; 1:283.

13   John Milton, *Paradise Lost: A Poem in Twelve Books, A New Edition with Notes of Various Authors, by Thomas Newton*, 2 vols. (London: J. and R. Tonson and S. Draper, 1749), 1:10.

Expatiate free o'er all this scene of Man;
A mighty maze! But not without a plan;
A Wild, where weeds and flow'rs promiscuous shoot,
Or Garden, tempting with forbidden fruit. . . .

Laugh where we must, be candid where we can;
But vindicate the ways of God to Man.

(lines 3–16)

Pope himself fudges the issue in his manuscript notes to the poem, reading his own final line as if it were Milton's: "The last line sums up the moral and main Drift of the whole, [the?] Justification of the Ways of Provi[dence]."[14]

Johnson knows the difference: he quotes Milton's line nearly correctly, but changes "man" for "men" in "And justify the ways of God to man," in the quotation illustrating the use of the noun ARGUMENT in the *Dictionary*'s first and fourth editions. He also quotes Pope's lines correctly, with the proper attribution, to provide an example of typeface in the *Dictionary*'s first and fourth editions, for BURGEOIS, "2. A type of a particular sort, probably so called from him who first used it, as," followed by Pope's couplet in Burgeois type. This noteworthy example suggests that Johnson uncharacteristically chose the widely recognized quotation from memory, since it does not contain the word exemplified.

It would be overstating the likelihood to claim that Johnson is intentionally refashioning Milton's *Paradise Lost* and its theology in the image of Pope and the *Essay on Man*. Yet there is considerable evidence of Johnson's literal ambivalence towards Milton and his own attempts to reduce and alter Milton's voice. In the cases I have cited, Johnson seems to be reading Milton, probably unconsciously, through the experience of Pope's poem. If nothing else, these instances attest to the power of texts to penetrate consciousness and become ineradicably part of one's reading and thinking. He has read Milton through Pope's Deistic, ultimately unsympathetic eyes. It is worth mentioning that in the case of the illustration for VINDICATE, the passage with Pope's line attributed to Milton, we can be fairly sure that Johnson quoted from memory, rather than mis-transcribed, for the actual word illustrated is not otherwise found in the original text, only in his own misremembering.

14   Alexander Pope, *An Essay on Man*, ed. Maynard Mack (London: Methuen, 1950), 12. In a private communication, Howard Weinbrot has pointed out that Pope probably uses "vindicate" in a Latin sense, from *vindicare*, suggesting the relevant meaning of "to set free." "Vindicat[ing] the ways of God to man" thus frees God from blame for man's miserable, self-induced state. Johnson's misquoting of Milton under VINDICATE, def. 4, "To clear; to protect from censure," would seem to corroborate this understanding of the word. If this is a correct reading, Pope's line does not directly contradict Milton's, yet it does offer a different interpretation of Milton's invocation from that apparently intended by the author.

Does Johnson really see Milton through a filter of Pope? It is worth considering, especially in light of the strange addition to the revised edition of the *Dictionary* under To LOSE v.a.: Johnson adds a new definition 2, as follows: "To forfeit as a penalty. In this sense is Paradise *lost*." Illustrating this new definition is not a quotation from Milton, but one adapted from Pope's "Temple of Fame" (ll, 502–504): "Fame—few, alas! the casual blessing boast,/So hard to gain, so easy to be *lost*! *Pope*." Johnson seems to go to some length to "re-place" Milton literally with Pope and his poetic lines.

Johnson redeems Milton from his dark historical role, and in this respect, he disembodies him, instating him instead as the timeless sacred poet. Yet even in his poetic role, Milton appears—in these cases, at least—to be challenged and critiqued by the younger poet Pope. How far can or should we go in interpreting evidence from John Milton in the *Dictionary* or from any of the quoted authorities? Robert Folkenflik has recently written, "We can safely say what the *Dictionary* thinks; it is more difficult to make claims about what Johnson thinks on the basis of *Dictionary* illustrations or even definitions."[15] Whether or not we can agree on what "the *Dictionary* thinks," we should follow Folkenflik's skepticism in drawing unwarranted conclusions about Johnson from the text. Nevertheless, we may glimpse apparent patterns of Johnson's thought, intentions, and execution within the intertextualities of *A Dictionary of the English Language*.

15   Robert Folkenflik, "The Politics of Johnson's *Dictionary* Revisited," *The Age of Johnson* 18 (2007): 11.

Modes of Definition in Johnson
and His Contemporaries

Jack Lynch

There has long been a kind of sport in Johnsonian circles—the game of catching Johnson out and reveling in his failed predictions. Perhaps the most famous of these misfires is his opinion of Sterne: "Nothing odd will do long. 'Tristram Shandy' did not last."[1] That line decorates the jackets of several editions of Sterne's famously eccentric book; fans of Sterne enjoy gloating over how far wrong the Great Cham could be. At least one of Johnson's false predictions, though, has not attracted much attention. "That part of my work on which I expect malignity most frequently to fasten," Johnson wrote in the Preface to his *Dictionary* (1755), "is the *Explanation*."[2] In fact surprisingly few commentators have fastened malignity—or even attention—on Johnson's "explanations," or, as we would say, definitions.

That is not to say there has been *no* attention, or no malignity. There were objections to his definitions from the beginning. Charles Richardson, under the influence of the cranky John Horne Tooke, complained at great length about Johnson's definitions, and found his methods "a short and infallible recipe to write sheer nonsense."[3] Noah Webster was another lexicographer who felt Horne Tooke's influence: in 1809 he wrote that "Even the definitions, which constitute the whole value of *Johnson's* Dictionary, are deficient in precision beyond any thing I could have imagined without a minute attention to the subject."[4] Richardson and Webster, though, were unusual in the attention they paid to the subject.

A Victorian tradition of praising Johnson's definitions nonetheless countered the complaints of Richardson and Webster. Thomas Carlyle, for instance, noted, "Had

---

1 *Boswell's Life of Johnson. Together with Boswell's Journal of a Tour to the Hebrides and Johnson's Diary of a Journey into North Wales*, ed. George Birkbeck Hill, rev. L. F. Powell, 6 vols. (Oxford: Clarendon Press, 1934–1964), 2:449.

2 Samuel Johnson, Preface to the *Dictionary*, in *Johnson on the English Language*, in *The Yale Edition of the Works of Samuel Johnson*, ed. Gwin J. Kolb and Robert DeMaria Jr., vol. 18 (New Haven: Yale University Press, 2005), 88 (hereafter cited as *Johnson on the English Language*).

3 Charles Richardson, *Illustrations of English Philology* (London: Printed for Gale and Fenner, 1815), 15.

4 Webster to Thomas Davies, July 25, 1809, in *Letters of Noah Webster*, ed. Harry R. Warfel (New York: Library Publishers, 1953), 323.

Johnson left nothing but his *Dictionary*, one might have traced there a great intellect, a genuine man. Looking to its clearness of definition, its general solidity, honesty, insight and successful method, it may be called the best of all Dictionaries." Even Macaulay was uncharacteristically generous toward Johnson: "The definitions," he wrote, "show so much acuteness of thought and command of language, and the passages quoted from poets, divines, and philosophers are so skilfully selected, that a leisure hour may always be very agreeably spent in turning over the pages."[5] George Alfred Stringer praised "the nice discrimination with which each word in Johnson's Dictionary is defined and illustrated." He concluded that "Studied from *any* point of view the Dictionary is a wonderful treasury, and in many respects it will never again be equalled, certainly never excelled."[6] In a lecture delivered in 1967, J. P. Hardy continued the Victorian tradition of belletristic commendation: "Anyone who uses Johnson's *Dictionary* will find that its level of performance in definition is, for the most part, exceedingly high."[7] Elizabeth Hedrick sums up the conventional wisdom when she says the definitions are "generally considered the *Dictionary*'s great strength."[8]

Most such panegyrics, though, are subjective and impressionistic; few explain what constitutes a good definition, or even compare Johnson's definitions with those of his predecessors, contemporaries, or successors. Both scholarly and belletristic modern readers certainly enjoy focusing on his quirky definitions: the personal ones like *lexicographer* and *grubstreet*, the political ones like *Whig* and *excise*, the wrong ones like *pastern* and *leeward*, the incomprehensible ones like *cough* and *network* are familiar to many who have never given serious thought to the *Dictionary*. But even experts pay little attention to the tens of thousands of ordinary definitions. There has been abundant commentary on Johnson's illustrative quotations, on the corpus or canon of authors on whom he drew, on his usage notes, on his place on the descriptive–prescriptive continuum, on his treatment of obsolete words, on his attitudes toward cant and orality, even on his notoriously weak etymologies. Some of the better criticism of the *Dictionary* has tried to extract a theory of language from Johnson's practice, and to identify the works that most influenced him, John Locke and Isaac Watts above

5   Thomas Carlyle, "The Hero as Man of Letters," in *Heroes, Hero-Worship, & the Heroic in History*, ed. Michael K. Goldberg, Joel J. Brattin, and Mark Engel (Berkeley and Los Angeles: University of California Press, 1993), 157; Thomas Babington Macaulay, *Essay on Johnson*, ed. Samuel Thurber and Louise Wetherbee (Boston: Allyn and Bacon, 1924), 25.

6   George Alfred Stringer, *Leisure Moments in Gough Square; or, The Beauties and Quaint Conceits of Johnson's Dictionary* (Buffalo, N.Y.: Ulbrich & Kingsley, 1886), 11.

7   J. P. Hardy, *"Dictionary" Johnson* (Armidale, N.S.W.: University of New England, 1967), 6.

8   Elizabeth Hedrick, "Locke's Theory of Language and Johnson's *Dictionary*," *Eighteenth-Century Studies* 20, no. 4 (Summer 1987): 422–444, at 424. I owe a particular debt of gratitude to Hedrick, whose comments on an earlier version of this essay proved valuable in reworking it.

all.[9] Nevertheless, the specific techniques he used to define words have received little scrutiny.

Johnsonians, then, whether amateur or professional, have paid surprisingly little attention to Johnson's definitions. Conversely, experts in definition have paid surprisingly little attention to Johnson. He rarely shows up in modern linguistic discussions of definition, except as part of a quick glance back at the inchoate prehistory of serious lexicography. Johnson's name appears nowhere in Juan C. Sager's *Essays on Definition*, for instance, and he gets just a quick tip of the hat in Ladislav Zgusta's *Manual of Lexicography* and Sidney I. Landau's *Dictionaries*.[10] Henri Béjoint notes that in early dictionaries, "the frequent words were treated with an economy of style that looks strange to our modern eyes," and adduces as an example Johnson's definition of *fish* as simply "an animal that inhabits the water."[11] *The Oxford Guide to Practical Lexicography* includes a sidebar, "Defining in Dictionaries: A Brief History," that places Johnson in an era when "defining styles had not yet been standardized and were quite heterogeneous." The authors are content to praise him because he "ended up with a realistic appreciation of the limits of lexicography, and he saw his task as a practical one."[12] Several lexicographers and lexicologists note that Johnson was among the first to state explicitly the principle that noun phrases should be interpreted in the form of noun phrases, verbs in the form of verbs, and so on—"The rigour of interpretative lexicography requires that the explanation, and the word explained, should be always reciprocal"—but only a few have paid any attention to whether he makes good on his promise.[13]

Scholars know what many beginning students do not—that dictionaries contain much more than just definitions—and those other aspects of Johnson's *Dictionary* have been well documented. But surely it is noteworthy that the profession has neglected the subject of definition so thoroughly. A review of the scholarship on the subject is largely a review of its absence. Although the word *definition* appears in any number

9   The two best overviews on this subject are Robert DeMaria Jr., "The Theory of Language in Johnson's *Dictionary*," in *Johnson after Two Hundred Years*, ed. Paul J. Korshin (Philadelphia: University of Pennsylvania Press, 1986), 159–174, and Hedrick, "Locke's Theory of Language." See also Rackstraw Downes, "Johnson's Theory of Language," *Review of English Literature* 3 (October 1962): 29–41.

10   See Juan C. Sager, ed., *Essays on Definition* (Amsterdam and Philadelphia: J. Benjamins, 2000); Ladislav Zgusta, *Manual of Lexicography* (Prague: Academia; The Hague: Mouton, 1971); and Sidney I. Landau's *Dictionaries: The Art and Craft of Lexicography* (New York: Scribner, 1984).

11   Henri Béjoint, *Modern Lexicography: An Introduction* (Oxford: Oxford University Press, 1994), 96.

12   B. T. Sue Atkins and Michael Rundell, *The Oxford Guide to Practical Lexicography* (Oxford: Oxford University Press, 2008), 432.

13   See, for example, Robert Ilson, *Lexicography: An Emerging International Profession* (Manchester: Manchester University Press, 1986), 117.

of articles on Johnson, it is almost always either metaphorical, as in *self-definition*, or merely evocative, as in *the definition of brilliant*. Robert DeMaria's *Johnson's Dictionary and the Language of Learning*—an epochal work, which can be said to have begun the modern study of the book—has no index entry for *definition*. This is hardly a failing, since DeMaria does more than his share of important things, but it is revealing. Allen Reddick's similarly influential *Making of Johnson's Dictionary, 1746–1773* has an entry for *definitions, Johnson's system of*, but it gets only a smattering of page references. This is true as well for the collection Anne McDermott and I edited in 2005, *Anniversary Essays on Johnson's* Dictionary.

The result is the counterintuitive situation in which very few have paid attention to Johnson's *Dictionary* for the things most everyday users seek in a dictionary—the definitions. Odd as it sounds, other than the famous Preface, the part of Johnson's *Dictionary* that has received the least critical attention is the part he actually wrote himself.

There is one extended discussion of Johnson's definitions, though it never appeared in print: Jeffrey T. Gross's University of Virginia dissertation of 1975.[14] Gross's interest is in Johnson's definitions of common words, especially phrasal verbs, and he devotes particular attention to Johnson's attempts to surmount some of the perennial problems that face lexicographers. Among published criticism, one article stands out, James McLaverty's "From Definition to Explanation" (1986). McLaverty relates Johnson's definitions to a debate between Watts and Locke on the nature of language.[15]

I would like to encourage more attention to Johnson's habits in defining—how, in short, does he define words? How, then, should we talk about definitions?—what is there to say about them? Since the question has largely gone unasked, and it is unclear what form an answer would take, my arguments here can be nothing more than tentative. I offer my conclusions in the hope of encouraging further discussion.

---

14   Jeffrey T. Gross, "The Process of Definition in Dr. Johnson's Dictionary: The Poet, Philosopher, and Moralist as Lexicographer" (PhD diss., University of Virginia, 1975). Only one article, "Dr. Johnson's Treatment of English Particles in the *Dictionary*," *University of Mississippi Studies in English* 2 (1981): 71–92, was drawn from it.

15   James McLaverty, "From Definition to Explanation: Locke's Influence on Johnson's Dictionary," *Journal of the History of Ideas* 47, no. 3 (1986): 377–394 . Another brief but relevant discussion appeared in the same year: DeMaria's "Theory of Language in Johnson's *Dictionary*," esp. 168–169. There are, of course, discussions of specific definitions and kinds of definitions. Kathleen Wales discusses Johnson's use of synonymy in "Johnson's Use of Synonyms in Dictionary and Prose Style: The Influence of John Locke?," *Prose Studies* 8, no. 1 (1985): 25–34; Silvia Cacchiani looks at intensifiers in "Desperately, Utterly and Other Intensifiers: On Their Inclusion and Definition in Dr Johnson's *Dictionary*," *Textus: English Studies in Italy* 19, no. 1 (2006): 217–236. See also Chris P. Pearce, "Recovering the 'Rigour of Interpretive Lexicography': Border Crossings in Johnson's *Dictionary*," *Textus: English Studies in Italy* 19, no. 1 (2006): 33–50.

One might begin with the questions that twentieth- and twenty-first-century lexicographers consider the most important aspects of definition, but many of the concerns of modern linguists were not germane in an eighteenth-century context. Such an approach would necessarily be ahistorical, and would amount to judging the past according to how well it lives up to the standards of the present. On the other hand, one might consider the theories about definition that circulated in Johnson's day, particularly what was called *logical definition*, derived from Scholastic notions and made newly relevant by many seventeenth-century English philosophers. As Sidney I. Landau points out, "Although the distinction is not always made, and when made not always observed, logical definition is not the same as lexical definition. Logical definition—Richard Robinson calls it real definition, because it attempts to analyze things in the real world, as distinguished from words—has been the chief preoccupation of philosophers."[16] This has the advantage of being historical, but the disadvantage of being too abstract to be genuinely useful—McLaverty has related Johnson's conceptions of linguistic "explanation" to philosophical "definition," but the idea is difficult to apply to many other kinds of definition in Johnson's *Dictionary*.

It seems the most responsible way to approach the question is by comparing Johnson's practice to that of other lexicographers.[17] I therefore describe some of the means lexicographers have used to define words, and then examine the frequency with which Johnson and the creators of other dictionaries used each of them. Before getting to the list, though, we might acknowledge some of Johnson's failures. "Some words there are which I cannot explain," Johnson frankly acknowledged in the Preface, "because I do not understand them."[18] Of *trolmydames*, he writes, "Of this word I know not the meaning"; *stammel*, likewise; or *etch*, "A country word, of which I know not the meaning"—here he is unambiguous about his shortcomings. He is similarly clear about his failure in producing some impenetrable definitions. Zgusta includes in his list of four fundamental principles of definition that "The lexical definition should not contain words 'more difficult to understand' than the word defined."[19] Johnson, however, knew full well that "To explain, requires the use of terms less abstruse than that which is to be explained, and such terms cannot always be found; for as nothing can be proved but by supposing something intuitively known, and evident without proof, so nothing can be defined but by the use of words too plain to admit a definition."[20]

Some of Johnson's definitions fail for another reason. Richardson, writing in *Illustrations of English Philology* (1815), was eager to point out Johnson's shortcomings.

16   Landau, "Dictionaries," 120.

17   These include Robert Cawdrey, Thomas Blount, Edward Phillips, John Kersey, Nathan Bailey, Benjamin Martin, John Ash, Noah Webster, and Charles Richardson. See note 39 for full bibliographical particulars.

18   *Johnson on the English Language*, 90.

19   Landau, "Dictionaries," 124.

20   *Johnson on the English Language*, 89.

"Are you in search of a short and infallible recipe to write sheer nonsense?" he asks. "I will present you with one in an instant.—'The rigour of interpretative lexicography, (says Johnson) requires that the explanation, and the word explained, should be reciprocal.' Obey this rule, in your use of his Dictionary, and your success is ensured. I will give you an instance;—That stumbling-block to all keen metaphysicians, the word CAUSE." Johnson's definition of *cause* is "that which produces or effects any thing." Then comes Johnson's definition of *to effect*: "To produce as a Cause." And then *to produce*: "To cause." "Substituting the explanations for the words explained," Richardson writes, "A Cause is, that which causes or causes as a cause—any thing." Richardson concludes, therefore, that "no man can possibly succeed in compiling a truly valuable Dictionary of the English Language, unless he entirely desert the steps of Johnson."[21]

Johnson, though, was well aware of these dangers, and needed no Richardson or Horne Tooke to point them out. "Some explanations," he wrote, "are unavoidably reciprocal or circular, as *hind, the female of the stag; stag, the male of the hind.*"[22] Even if we go beyond those narrowly circular definitions, we still run into the problem of circularity, because words are always necessarily defined in other words, all of which must be found in a dictionary. It is impossible to escape circularity altogether.[23] When the circle of definition is too narrow, though, the definition becomes useless. Richardson pointed out the narrow circle of *produce, cause,* and *effect*; there is an even narrower circle in the entry for *defluxion*, which Johnson unhelpfully defined as "a defluxion."[24]

After these examples of failed definitions, though, we can turn our attention to those that make at least a pretense to a proper explanation. For these I would like to propose that there are at least nine modes of definition—not a comprehensive list, but this catalog can serve as a starting point for further discussion.

The first mode of definition may be the least interesting, but it forms a large part of almost every dictionary: it defines a word by referring to its obvious etymon

21   Richardson, *Illustrations of English Philology*, 15–17. In its form, Richardson's derision recalls Coleridge's contemporary taunt, reducing the opening couplet of *The Vanity of Human Wishes* to "Let Observation with extensive observation observe mankind extensively" (*Collected Letters of Samuel Taylor Coleridge*, ed. Earl Leslie Griggs, 6 vols. [Oxford: Clarendon Press, 1956–1971], 4:685). Reducing a lexicographer to tautology seems to be a particularly effective put-down.

22   *Johnson on the English Language*, 93.

23   Compare Béjoint: "Circularity is inevitable, particularly for the definitions of very frequent words, and especially of function words, as Samuel Johnson had already noticed in the Preface to his dictionary. The only thing the lexicographer can do is avoid the simplest types, like A = A, or A = B and B = A. The longer type, A = B, B = N, and N = A, is unavoidable" (*Modern Lexicography*, 203). We might add, as an extreme example, that the *Oxford English Dictionary* includes dozens of occurrences of forms of *to be* in the definition for *be* v.

24   He goes on to add, "a flowing down of humours." He was not alone in this kind of definition; Bailey defined *nail* as "the nail of a man's hand."

and offering a mechanical glossing of its affixes. These are typically introduced by a few simple formulas, such as "the quality or condition of being" such-and-such. For example, one might define *national* as "related to the nation," *nationalize* as "to make national," or *nationally* as "in a national manner." These definitions rarely tell us anything we did not know already; they are little more than signs pointing to other definitions, and are usually included only to demonstrate that a word exists, or to provide an opportunity to give pronunciations, illustrative quotations, and the other kinds of material dictionaries often provide. The alternative, however, is to repeat the substantial part of the root's definition in every entry, as when John Ash defines *narrate* as "to relate, to tell," *narrated* as "related, told," *narrating* as "relating, telling," and *narrator* as "one that relates." Most dictionaries, viewing that sort of repetition as a waste of space, often resort to definitions that refer to the entry of the etymon.

The second, and probably the most obvious, mode of definition is more satisfactory, but still poses its own problems. It is the single synonym: the suggestion is that the word being defined, the *definiendum*, can be replaced unproblematically with the single word doing the defining, the *definiens*. Johnson often resorts to these when he defines inkhorn terms, as in his definition of *puniceous* as "purple," or *cephalalgy* as "the headach." Such definitions are often convenient for associating an obscure word with a more familiar one, but there are several substantial problems with using synonyms in definitions. The first problem is, as Johnson wrote in the Preface, that "Words are seldom exactly synonimous; a new term was not introduced, but because the former was thought inadequate."[25] He also noted that the subtle differences between apparent synonyms are important: "The difference of signification in words generally accounted synonimous, ought to be carefully observed; as in *pride, haughtiness, arrogance*."[26]

Even if we could find two words that are perfectly interchangeable in one sense, at least one of them is likely to be polysemous, and they will almost never coincide in *all* their meanings. As Landau points out, "One cannot define *backyard* . . . by the English word *lot*, since *lot* has a lot of other meanings."[27] Atkins and Rundell maintain "there is a fundamental objection to defining by synonym, namely, that no two words are exactly alike. True synonymy . . . entails complete interchangeability in every possible context of use."[28] Locke even writes that "*a Definition is* nothing else, but *the shewing the meaning of one Word by several other not synonymous Terms*." He dismisses the definition of *motion* as "passage" by saying "This is to translate, and not to define," charging those who would write such a definition with "put[ting] one synonymous Word for another."[29]

25   *Johnson on the English Language*, 91.

26   Ibid., 18:49. See also Wales, "Johnson's Use of Synonyms," 27.

27   Landau, "Dictionaries," 138.

28   Atkins and Rundell, 421.

29   John Locke, *Essay concerning Human Understanding*, ed. Peter H. Nidditch (Oxford: Clarendon Press, 1975), 3.4.6 (422) and 3.4.9 (423).

Somewhat more sophisticated, and often more satisfying, than a single synonym is a small number of synonyms, as with Johnson's definition of *computer* as "Reckoner; accountant; calculator." A naive assumption might be that these three synonyms of the *definiendum* must all be synonymous, not only with the *definiendum* but with one another. I suspect few actual dictionary users, however, make this assumption in practice. More likely they understand that the *definiendum* is not exactly the same as any of the offered *definientia*, but that its meaning can be discerned in the points at which those other words, though perhaps polysemous themselves, overlap. When Johnson defines *patron* n.s. 3 as "Advocate; defender; vindicator," he does not suggest that *patron* shares all the meanings of *advocate*, all the meanings of *defender*, and all the meanings of *vindicator*; instead he points in the direction of the meaning or meanings shared by all three words. An *advocate* might be a lawyer, a *defender* might be warrior, and a *vindicator* might be the author of a theodicy; but a *patron* is one who resides at the intersection of those three polysemous terms. Johnson makes extensive use of this mode, as when he defines *name* n.s. 5 as "Renown; fame; celebrity; eminence; praise; remembrance; memory; distinction; honour."[30] Sometimes, as here, the words seem to be the result of free-form brainstorming, but Johnson was sometimes explicit about drawing synonyms from two language families: "I have endeavoured frequently to join a *Teutonick* and *Roman* interpretation, as to CHEER, to *gladden*, or *exhilarate*, that every learner of *English* may be assisted by his own tongue."[31]

Multiple synonyms are not always easy to count, particularly with polysemous words. Since Benjamin Martin was the only lexicographer before Johnson to number senses, it is often difficult to tell whether a list of words in a definition is really to be understood as a series of synonyms, or a number of distinct senses. In Thomas Blount's definition of *navitie* as "diligence, stirring, quickness," is the reader meant to understand that *navitie* has three distinct meanings—(1) diligence; (2) stirring; (3) quickness—or that it has a single meaning, understood as the intersection of those three terms? When Phillips defines *naiant* as "swimming or floating," are we to understand these as two distinct possibilities, applying to both swimming things and floating things, or as a pair of words that seek to approximate a single sense? It is not always easy to tell, and I have often had to make judgment calls about how best to classify a definition. In the first set of tallies, I will consider both varieties of the synonymous definition as one mode.[32]

---

30   See Wales: Johnson "makes use of a greater number of synonyms in his definitions" than his contemporaries ("Johnson's Use of Synonyms," 27).

31   *Johnson on the English Language*, 93.

32   In order to justify my treating single and multiple synonyms as a single mode, I anticipate some of my conclusions by noting that Johnson's handling of single versus multiple synonyms is in keeping with the practice of the other lexicographers. Johnson uses synonyms of any sort in 45 percent of his definitions in the sample beginning with *na-* considered below; 7 percent of those definitions are nothing but a single synonym. Benjamin Martin gives the same figures; for Bailey they are 25 percent and 7 percent respectively,

A third mode of definition, and one closely related to the synonym, is the antonym. I include in this category definitions that are defined in terms of a lack or want, as when *nameless* is defined as "without a name," and *ablepsy* as "want of sight." Words with privative affixes are obvious candidates for this sort of definition by antonym, as when *unorthodox* is defined in negative terms as "Not holding pure doctrine," or *nonconformity* as "Refusal of compliance." But many other kinds of words lend themselves to definitions of this sort, and even seemingly positive terms can be defined as the antonyms of related negative terms. Thus Johnson defines one sense of *natural* with the explanation "Not forced; not farfetched," and *real* adj. 2 is "Not fictitious; not imaginary."

The fourth and fifth modes form a pair. For some noun phrases—especially human artifacts, though also some natural phenomena—it is possible to describe their components, their purposes, or both. When Johnson defines *oxymel* as "A mixture of vinegar and honey" he describes the parts; when he defines *picktooth* as "An instrument by which the teeth are cleaned," he describes the function; when he defines *gawntree* as "A wooden frame on which beer-casks are set when tunned," he gives both the mode of construction and the purpose for which it was created. The definition of *paper* n.s. 1—"Substance on which men write and print; made by macerating linen rags in water, and then spreading them in thin sheets"—is a good example of a definition that indicates both the purpose and the manner in which paper is created.

The sixth mode, the most demanding of all, is known as *genus–differentia* definition, and it has received the most extensive scholarly commentary because of its deep history in philosophy. Its origin is Aristotle's *Posterior Analytics*: "it is right when any one is conversant with a certain whole, to divide the genus into the individuals which are first in species, . . . then to endeavour thus to assume the definitions of these."[33] Lexicographers had no need to learn this lesson directly from Aristotle; it was recycled by many Scholastic thinkers, and resurfaced among seventeenth-century philosophers including Isaac Watts. Locke was explicit about its applicability to lexicography: "*in the defining of Words*, which is nothing but declaring their signification, *we make use of the Genus*, or next general Word that comprehends it. Which is not out of necessity, but only to save the labour of enumerating the several simple *Ideas*, which the next general Word, or *Genus*, stands for."[34]

and for John Ash 44 percent and 12 percent respectively. Johnson uses multiple synonyms in 23 percent of his definitions, compared to 12 percent in Bailey, 27 percent in Martin, 18 percent in Ash, 41 percent in Webster's *Compendious Dictionary*, and 20 percent in Webster's *American Dictionary*. In 20 percent of his definitions, Johnson combines synonymy with some other mode of definition. This, too, is in keeping with his contemporaries: 12 percent in Martin, 22 percent in Ash, 29 percent in the *Compendious Dictionary*, and 18 percent in the *American Dictionary*.

33   *Posterior Analytics* 2.13, in *The Organon, or Logical Treatises, of Aristotle*, trans. Octavius Freire Owen, 2 vols. (London, 1853).

34   Locke, *Essay*, 3.3.10 (412–413).

James McLaverty describes Watts's influence on Johnson on this point in particular: the best way to ensure that definitions are "reciprocal with the Thing defined" and that "the *Definition* may be used in any sentence in the Place of the *Thing defined*" is "*per genus et differentiam*—the method used by Wilkins in drawing up his tables."[35] In this kind of definition the lexicographer, confronted with a word, gives the kind of thing, the *genus*, to which the word belongs, and then provides one or more *differentiae* to distinguish this particular thing from others. (Modern lexicographers sometimes use the terms *hypernym* and *hyponym* to make the same distinction.) Johnson does this with many words: the *moose* is "The large American deer," which places the animal in its kind (*deer*), and tells us it is unlike other deer because it is large and American; an *opiate* is "A medicine that causes sleep," which tells us the kind of thing it is (*a medicine*) and its particular somnific powers that distinguish it from other medicines. And while it is easiest to do this with substantives, especially concrete nouns, it can be done with verbs as well, as when Johnson defines *prate* as "To talk carelessly [*sic*] and without weight": prating is talking, but a particular kind of talking.[36]

As a coda to the description of *genus–differentia* definitions, it is worth noting that some of Johnson's definitions consist of nothing but a genus—and these, we have to admit, are among the weakest definitions in the book. To learn that a *trocar* is "A chirurgical instrument" leaves us little wiser than when we began; likewise *gavot*, which is "A kind of dance," or *traytrip*, which is "A kind of play, I know not of what kind." I call this genus-only style a seventh mode.

I conclude my catalog with two more varieties. Mode number eight is to define a word by not defining it at all—rather, letting someone else define it. Johnson sometimes allows his quotations to do his defining, particularly when he copies definitions directly out of encyclopedias. Of course we should remember that Johnson almost always wanted his quotations to supplement his definitions. As he put it in the Preface, after dwelling on the challenges of producing useful definitions, "The solution of all difficulties, and the supply of all defects, must be sought in the examples."[37] Those who point gleefully to the curt definition of *Whig* as "The name of a faction" often neglect the 170-word quotation from Burnet that follows. Under this rubric I count those that include no original definition at all, and depend entirely on another writer to do the explaining.

Finally, I am left with mode number nine, a miscellaneous catch-all of "other," since no finite list of modes of definition could hope to be comprehensive. Perhaps

35   McLaverty, "From Definition to Explanation," 381.

36   As Atkins and Rundell put it, this kind of definition works with "many classes of verb, including verbs of motion (thus *trudge*, *tiptoe*, and *stroll* can all be defined using the genus 'walk'), verbs of making or creating (*reproduce*, *photocopy*, and *forge* can all be defined with the genus 'copy', which is itself a hyponym of 'make' or 'create'), and several others." *The Oxford Guide*, 415.

37   *Johnson on the English Language*, 93.

another critic will extend my study by distinguishing some of these miscellaneous modes more precisely.

Having distinguished these nine classes, I should add that they are not always clearly demarcated. A synonym with an *un-* prefix might just as easily be seen as an antonym; a short noun phrase in a definition—say, defining *nacre* as "mother of pearl"—might be treated as a synonym if we focus on it as a single verbal unit, or as another kind of definition if we regard it as separate words tied together syntactically. What is more, the various modes need not be mutually exclusive. Johnson very often defines a word or sense using several of these methods at once. In defining *omelet* as "A kind of pancake made with eggs" he gives us the genus and its components. The eighth sense of the noun *name* shows three of these modes in just five words: "Appearance; not reality; assumed character." There we have a synonym, an antonym, and a genus–differentia definition. (This is why, in the table below, the totals across the columns always add up to more than 100 percent—if a word is defined with several methods, it is counted several times.)

Having created this list, I now suggest what to do with it. Since it is impossible to say on an *a priori* basis how common each of these nine modes should be, it seems most productive to compare Johnson's practice with that of the other lexicographers of his day—and, since that pool is limited, with the creators of the other major English monolingual dictionaries before the rise of scientific philology late in the nineteenth century. Some rudimentary numerical analysis may prove valuable.

Genuinely reliable numerical comparison of the defining habits of various dictionaries is probably impossible. The first reason is that dictionaries take different approaches toward the kinds of words they include: Ash, for instance, includes many proper names (*Nahum, Nabonassar, Narbarth*) and many inflected forms (*narrow, narrowed, narrower, narrowest, narrowing*) as separate headwords; Johnson does not.[38] And some lexicographers give just one sense for each lemma—Martin and Johnson begin the systematic practice of numbered senses—whereas earlier lexicographers tend to lump many senses together, sometimes separating them with semicolons, but often just running them together into one long definition. Consider the word *narration*: Cawdrey defines one sense in three words, Kersey discusses two senses in a total of twenty-seven words, and Bailey identifies five distinct senses in two hundred twenty-nine words. They are not really comparable. Moreover, quantitative methods can tell us nothing about qualitative matters. A table can tell us whether a lexicographer had recourse to synonyms, but it cannot tell us whether those synonyms were well chosen.

---

38   Ash also often lists proper names twice, once as a noun, once as an adjective: *Namptwich*, substantive, "A town in Cheshire"; *Namptwich*, adjective, "Belonging to Namptwich; made at Namptwich." Even Johnson, though, was aware of the difficulties of distinguishing senses; in the Preface he writes that "kindred senses may be so interwoven, that the perplexity cannot be disentangled." *Johnson on the English Language*, 91.

It can tell us nothing about whether a definition is clear, elegant, or even minimally accurate. Any numbers we derive from comparisons, therefore, may be thought-provoking, but it makes no sense to report them to six significant digits.

Still, with all these caveats, can we say anything about Johnson's practice and how it compares to that of other early lexicographers? Here I report the results of some tallies of the frequency of each of these nine types of definition in Johnson and ten other important early modern dictionaries, from Cawdrey in 1604 to Richardson's second edition of 1844.[39] It would be best to compare like with like, but the diversity of the dictionaries makes this impossible: the wordlists differ too much from dictionary to dictionary to allow us to look at the same words in all eleven dictionaries. But we can compare representative samples. The accompanying table gives my counts of each of the nine modes of definition in each of the eleven dictionaries for all the words or numbered senses beginning with the letters *na-*.

Why *na-*? That range has a few advantages.[40] It is long enough to give reliable results without being so long that counts are impractical. It contains a good mix of

39   The works cited: Robert Cawdrey, *A Table Alphabeticall, Conteyning and Teaching the True Writing, and Vnderstanding of Hard Vsuall English Words, Borrowed from the Hebrew, Greeke, Latine, or French, &c. with the Interpretation Thereof by Plaine English Words* (London: I. R[oberts], 1604); Thomas Blount, *Glossographia; or, A Dictionary, Interpreting All Such Hard Words, Whether Hebrew, Greek, Latin, Italian, Spanish, French, Teutonick, Belgick, British or Saxon; as Are Now Used in Our Refined English Tongue* (London: Tho. Newcomb, 1656); Edward Phillips, *The New World of English Words; or, A General Dictionary: Containing the Interpretations of Such Hard Words as Are Derived from Other Languages; Whether Hebrew, Arabick, Syriack, Greek, Latin, Italian, French, Spanish, British, Dutch, Saxon, &c.* (London: E. Tyler, 1658); John Kersey, *A New English Dictionary; or, A Compleat Collection of the Most Proper and Significant Words, Commonly Used in the Language* (London, 1702); Nathan Bailey, *Dictionarium Britannicum; or, A More Compleat Universal Etymological English Dictionary than Any Extant*, 2nd ed. (London: T. Cox, 1736); Benjamin Martin, *Lingua Britannica Reformata; or, A New English Dictionary . . . to Which Is Prefix'd, an Introduction, Containing a Physico-Grammatical Essay on the Propriety and Rationale of the English Tongue* (London, 1749); John Ash, *The New and Complete Dictionary of the English Language: In Which All the Words Are Introduced, the Different Spellings Preserved, the Sound of the Letters Occasionally Distinguished, the Obsolete and Uncommon Words Supported by Authorities, and the Different Construction and Uses Illustrated by Examples* (London: E. and C. Dilly, 1775); Noah Webster, *A Compendious Dictionary of the English Language: In Which Five Thousand Words Are Added to the Number Found in the Best English Compends* (New Haven: Hudson & Goodwin, 1806); Noah Webster, *An American Dictionary of the English Language*, 2 vols. (New York: S. Converse, 1828); Charles Richardson, *A New Dictionary of the English Language: To Which Is Prefixed a Grammatical and Etymological Examination Adapted to the Dictionary*, 2nd ed. (London, 1844). I do not provide a tally of etymological definitions for Richardson's *New Dictionary*, since every entry is structured around the etymon.

40   I use the same range, for many of the same reasons, in *The Age of Elizabeth in the Age of Johnson* (Cambridge: Cambridge University Press, 2003), 186.

parts of speech, a mix of commonplace words and inkhorn terms, a mix of the concrete and the abstract, a mix of words derived from Germanic and Romance roots, as well as directly from Latin and Greek, and a mix of monosemous and richly polysemous words. There are no prefixes (*electro-*, *micro-*) to distort the tallies. The *na-* range has one other strong advantage: by the middle of the alphabet, lexicographers have usually worked out their principles and procedures, whereas early letters often show the signs of improvisation.

The results of my counts are presented in the following table.

	Etymon	Synonym(s)	Antonym	Parts	Purpose	Genus–Diff	Genus	Quote	Other
Cawdrey 6 entries		50%							83%
Blount 34 entries	3%	36%		6%		21%			50%
Phillips 37 entries		24%				19%			65%
Kersey 54 entries	9%	37%	4%	7%		15%	7%		28%
Bailey 197 entries	4%	25%	2%	5%	3%	29%	4%	<1%	43%
Martin 97 entries	2%	45%	6%	4%	2%	23%	2%		34%
Johnson 196 entries	6%	45%	13%	1%	2%	17%	2%	4%	32%
Ash 277 entries	9%	44%	3%	3%	2%	31%	5%	<1%	33%
Webster 1 98 entries	5%	55%	6%	1%	1%	20%	5%		40%
Webster 2 306 entries	5%	34%	6%	2%	1%	15%	2%	8%	58%
Richardson 44 entries	–	41%	2%	9%	2%	18%	2%	9%	39%

Several things are evident at once. The first is that, with few exceptions, Johnson is rarely out of step in almost every category. His modes of definition are roughly similar to those of the other major lexicographers working from 1604 to 1844. If Johnson deserves praise for better definitions than those of his contemporaries, it is not because he took a radically different approach.

The next observation derives from the first, and has to do with the extent of Johnson's influence on the lexicographical tradition. Critics have long argued over how much Johnson changed the way dictionaries were made: Did he in fact standardize spellings, as many histories of the language say he did? Did he establish a standard English, or arrest linguistic "decay"? Those questions are too large to answer here, but if these results can suggest anything about Johnson's influence on the modes of definition, it is that his influence was minimal. There is no obvious shift in modes of definition before and after Johnson. It is true that the careful discrimination of senses developed by Martin continued apace, so perhaps the increased attention to polysemy in dictionaries after 1755 can be partly attributed to him.[41] Likewise the use of illustrative quotations, common on the Continent but very rare in general English lexicography before Johnson, was an innovation that was genuinely influential. These, however, have little to do with the shape the definitions themselves took.

There are, however, a few departures from the norm, and they deserve attention. The first is Johnson's uncommon dependence on the antonym, which appears in roughly one out of seven or eight of his entries—more than twice the rate of any other lexicographer. This was evidently part of his conception of his task from the beginning. Even in the *Plan* he writes that he will have to "explain many words by their opposition to others; for contraries are best seen when they stand together."[42] I suggest that this is typical of one of the characteristics of Johnson's mind: he often tests propositions by testing them against their opposites. Although Johnson nowhere refers to *antonyms* (the *Oxford English Dictionary* says the word would not be coined until 1870), his writings are filled with words like *opposed*, *opposite*, *contrary*, and *contrariety*, and it suggests a fundamentally dialectical approach he took to knowledge. He even confessed to taking pleasure in proceeding by testing ideas against their opposites: as Sir John Hawkins recorded Johnson's words, "I dogmatise and am contradicted, and in this conflict of opinions and sentiments I find delight."[43] One of the reasons Boswell's *Life* is successful

41 The typography appropriate to numbered senses was also original with Johnson. As Paul Luna argues, "if we look at how the Dictionary's typography articulates its underlying structure, we can see that Johnson's page was genuinely innovative and set the standard for English dictionaries for a century." Paul Luna, "The Typographic Design of Johnson's *Dictionary*," in *Anniversary Essays on Johnson's* Dictionary, ed. Jack Lynch and Anne McDermott (Cambridge: Cambridge University Press, 2005), 175–197, at 175.

42 *Johnson on the English Language*, 50.

43 Sir John Hawkins, *The Life of Samuel Johnson, LL.D.*, ed. O M Brack Jr. (Athens: University of Georgia Press, 2009), 56.

as a literary document is that Boswell so often provides a foil for Johnson's mind. It would be interesting to see the total number of occurrences of the phrase "No, Sir," in the *Life of Johnson*; it certainly appears before many of the most famous ipse dixits. A more extensive exploration of Johnson and the antonym is certainly called for.

The second thing that emerges from this exercise is Johnson's comparative lack of interest in the genus–differentia style, which features in just 17 percent of entries—compared to 29 percent in Bailey, 23 percent in Martin, and 31 percent in Ash (though Webster and Richardson are comparable to Johnson's practice). This seems to confirm some of McLaverty's assertions: Johnson was more interested in linguistic "explanation," which comes from social convention, than in logical "definition," associated with Aristotelian and Scholastic philosophy. Locke recognized that, "though defining by the *Genus* may be the shortest way; yet, I think, it may be doubted, whether it be the best." He explicated what he called "the ordinary Definition of the Schools," only to assert that "Languages are not always so made, according to the Rules of Logick, that every term can have its signification, exactly and clearly expressed by two others."[44] On this point Johnson clearly sided with Locke.[45] He recognized that strictly logical definition is liable to mistakes on the lexicographer's part and confusion on the reader's part: "sometimes things may be made darker by definition. I see a cow. I define her, *Animal quadrupes ruminans cornutum*. But a goat ruminates, and a cow may have no horns. *Cow* is plainer."[46] McLaverty suggests that Johnson began with logical definitions as a goal, but was forced to abandon them: "It was definitions of this sort—'strictly logical'—that Johnson had once hoped to achieve, but hoped in vain, he tells us in the Preface."[47]

This essay remains preliminary and tentative, but I hope to suggest that quantitative analysis can help us to derive coherent theses out of a comparative analysis of Johnson's and other lexicographers' means of defining words. Whether the numbers I have come up with in this brief survey are representative of larger trends is not clear; my sample size is small, and others are free to question my classification of these hundreds of definitions. Many of them depend on judgment calls, and another reader, even one using the same categories I have spelled out, would come up with different figures. Attention to this sort of feature of the *Dictionary* nevertheless has the potential to

---

44   Locke, *Essay*, 3.3.10 (413).

45   McLaverty writes, "Johnson sided with Locke against Watts on the fundamental question of the extent of human knowledge." He shared Watts's view that "explanations *per genus et differentiam* were brief, perspicuous, and elegant, and he used one where he could, but he agreed with Locke that few things or ideas could be adequately defined because human knowledge is too limited: simple ideas are irreducible, mixed modes too complex, substances essentially unknown." He concludes that this is the reason for "the preference for the word *explanation* or *interpretation* in the *Dictionary*." McLaverty, "From Definition to Explanation," 389–390.

46   *Life*, 3:245.

47   McLaverty, "From Definition to Explanation," 381.

illuminate aspects of Johnson's modes of proceeding and his achievements, whether his presumed "theory of language" or his debt to particular earlier lexicographers. Numerical analysis cannot take the place of careful reading of Johnson's works, but I hope that it can help us be more precise when we declare that Johnson wrote "good" definitions.

Studies of Johnson's *Dictionary*, 1955–2009:
A Bibliography

Jack Lynch

This bibliography provides information on studies of Samuel Johnson's *Dictionary of the English Language* (1755) between 1955 and 2009, from the bicentenary of the work's publication to the tercentenary of the author's birth.[1] The *Dictionary* remains one of the most cited books of the eighteenth century. A staggering number of critical studies include at least passing comments on the *Dictionary*. The work shows up in nearly every discussion of Johnson, even the most superficial; to much of the world, he is the man who "wrote the first dictionary." Numerous scholarly books and essays approach their subject by way of a definition from the *Dictionary*. But the sheer size of the work—2,300 folio pages, 43,000 headwords, 115,000 quotations, and something like 3.5 million words of text—means few have read the *Dictionary* through, and only a small number of the articles that cite it add anything to our knowledge of the book.

Because so many critical studies cite the *Dictionary*, it would be impossible to compile a comprehensive list of scholarship that touches on it. This bibliography is therefore limited to the works that offer sustained attention to the work itself, its compilation, publication, or reception. I have excluded master's theses, online resources, unpublished conference papers, and most ephemera, printed announcements of events for the various Johnson Societies, posters, bookmarks, sales brochures, postcards, and so on. Still the range of works included is wide, taking in nearly four hundred books, journal articles, book chapters, contributions to Festschriften, and doctoral

1   In preparing this bibliography I have drawn on several other bibliographical sources. James Clifford and Donald J. Greene, *Samuel Johnson: A Survey and Bibliography of Critical Studies* (Minneapolis: University of Minnesota Press, 1970); Donald J. Greene and John A. Vance, *A Bibliography of Johnsonian Studies, 1970–1985* (Victoria: University of Victoria Press, 1987); and my own *Bibliography of Johnsonian Studies, 1986–1998* (New York: AMS Press, 2000) cover studies of all of Johnson's works, and I have extracted those that deal especially with the *Dictionary*. I have supplemented those extractions with material drawn from J. E. and Elizabeth C. Congleton, *Johnson's Dictionary: Bibliographical Survey 1746–1984 with Excerpts for All Entries* (Terre Haute, Ind.: Dictionary Society of North America, 1984). I have also browsed as many general critical studies and biographies of Johnson as I could, looking for chapters on the *Dictionary* not indexed in the usual bibliographies and databases. Finally, I am grateful to Allen Reddick for drawing my attention to works I would otherwise have missed.

dissertations. I have included works intended for both a scholarly and a popular readership. The bibliography even includes three television programs: a documentary, a public lecture, and an episode of the sitcom *Blackadder*.

Any survey of the scholarship on the *Dictionary* must start with a number of landmark studies. Six book-length works in particular reveal the broad contours of the last half-century of *Dictionary* criticism. In 1955, the bicentenary of the *Dictionary*'s appearance, James H. Sledd and Gwin J. Kolb published *Dr. Johnson's Dictionary: Essays in the Biography of a Book*. It is the earliest work listed in this bibliography because it is genuinely epochal: modern criticism of the *Dictionary* can be said to begin with it. Sledd and Kolb declare their intention to revise the conventional wisdom that had accumulated around the *Dictionary*. "In the last fifty years or so," they wrote, "a great deal has been learned about the rise of English philology, about English grammatical traditions, English ideas of language, and the development of lexicography in England. What is needed," they argued, "is an attempt to bring this new knowledge to bear on Johnson."[2] They do this in five chapters: two are on "Johnson's *Dictionary* and the Lexicographical Tradition," one looking backwards, one forwards; there is a chapter on the work's composition and publication; another on Johnson's relationship with Chesterfield; and another on the early editions of the *Dictionary*. Although some of their conclusions have been qualified, challenged, even disproved over the years, the book remains the essential starting point for any serious student of the *Dictionary*.

Since 1955 the volume of *Dictionary* scholarship has increased steadily, although more than three decades passed before the next essential book-length scholarly study appeared. In 1986 Robert DeMaria, Jr. published *Johnson's Dictionary and the Language of Learning*, the first systematic survey of the illustrative quotations. Johnson himself invited readers to give his quotations more than strictly linguistic significance: "When first I collected these authorities," Johnson writes in the Preface, "I was desirous that every quotation should be useful to some other end than the illustration of a word."[3] DeMaria works to identify those other ends, writing, "Although there are almost always philological reasons for his selections, there are usually other reasons as well, and these other reasons have most often to do with the contribution the quotation can make to useful knowledge."[4] Drawing on an electronic database of 23,000 records— an important example of humanities computing in the pre-Internet age—DeMaria discerns "an identifiable central cluster of concerns" in the *Dictionary* as a whole,

2   James H. Sledd and Gwin J. Kolb, *Dr. Johnson's Dictionary: Essays in the Biography of a Book* (Chicago: University of Chicago Press, 1955), 3.

3   Samuel Johnson, *Johnson on the English Language*, in *The Yale Edition of the Works of Samuel Johnson*, ed. Gwin J. Kolb and Robert DeMaria Jr., vol. 18 (New Haven: Yale University Press, 2005), 93 (hereafter cited as *Johnson on the English Language*).

4   Robert DeMaria Jr., *Johnson's Dictionary and the Language of Learning* (Chapel Hill: University of North Carolina Press, 1986), ix–x.

including "knowledge and ignorance, truth and probability, learning and education, language, religion and morality."[5]

Allen Reddick's *Making of Johnson's Dictionary, 1746–1773* appeared in 1990, with a revised edition in 1996. This is still by far the most comprehensive account of the composition and revision of the *Dictionary*. Reddick was the first scholar to make extensive use of the so-called Sneyd–Gimbel copy of the *Dictionary*—Sledd and Kolb were aware of its existence in 1955, but were not allowed to examine it closely—and the surviving manuscript material related to the revised fourth edition. Reddick later published this material in a carefully prepared facsimile, *Samuel Johnson's Unpublished Revisions*. In addition to tracing the publication history in unprecedented detail, Reddick paid particular attention to the revisions made to the fourth edition of the *Dictionary* (1773), and, like DeMaria, made arguments about the significance of the quotations and the kind of intelligence implied by their selection.

The full text of the *Dictionary* has never been printed in a critical edition, but the publication of the full text of the first and fourth editions on CD-ROM in 1996, edited by Anne McDermott, has transformed the study of the work. Critics who hoped to say something about the *Dictionary* once had three choices: to read every one of its 3.5 million words, something that would take months of devotion; to turn to specific entries, trying to find relevant material; or to browse, allowing serendipity to turn up entries of interest. With the fully searchable text of the CD-ROM, however, it became possible to formulate questions that had once been practically unanswerable. McDermott's searchable text allows researchers to accumulate quantitative evidence that would have been nearly impossible to compile. We can now make systematic surveys of, say, Johnson's use of Shakespeare, the frequency of usage notes, the patterns of biblical citation, the number of etymologies derived from Arabic, Johnson's selection of legal or scientific terms, and the like.

In 2005, the 250th anniversary of the *Dictionary*'s publication, *Anniversary Essays on Johnson's* Dictionary provided a forum for fourteen scholars to reflect on the scholarship to date and to approach the work from new angles. The editors wrote that

> DeMaria and Reddick inaugurated a new stage of serious study of the *Dictionary*, but much remains to be done. Most notably, there has still been relatively little attention to Johnson's *Dictionary* as a dictionary. Compared with the attention paid to literary texts, dictionaries in general have received very little bibliographical, textual, stemmatic, critical, theoretical, or historiographical scrutiny. And most of those who have written about the *Dictionary* are literary scholars, who tend to regard Johnson as a literary lexicographer.[6]

5   Ibid., x.

6   Jack Lynch and Anne McDermott, eds., *Anniversary Essays on Johnson's* Dictionary (Cambridge: Cambridge University Press, 2005), 3.

Contributors were therefore encouraged to read the *Dictionary* as a dictionary—to treat it not only as a work of literature but as a reference book intended for practical use—bringing to bear on it the methods not only of literary critics but also of bibliographers, book designers, corpus linguists, and lexicographers.

The most recent landmark *Dictionary* publication also appeared in 2005, volume 18 of *The Yale Edition of the Works of Samuel Johnson*. Although the full text of the *Dictionary* is omitted—"The body of the *Dictionary* falls outside the scope of the *Yale Edition* because of its vast size"[7]—the various paratexts appear in serious critical editions for the first time, including the "Short Scheme" of 1746 and the *Plan* of 1747, both transcribed and reproduced in facsimile of the manuscripts, the Preface of 1755, and the other front matter to the *Dictionary* in its various editions. A long introduction places Johnson's *Dictionary* in the context of English and European lexicography; substantial editorial introductions to each of the works included provide further information about the composition, publication, and reception of the various pieces. The editorial notes are particularly useful in identifying the sources of many obscure quotations and allusions that had long baffled Johnsonians.

These six major publications do not exhaust all the topics of interest to students of the *Dictionary*; more focused books, journal articles, and doctoral dissertations have other concerns, of which a few deserve mention here. For a long time one of the most common questions regarding Johnson's *Dictionary* was his originality—the degree to which he could be said to have introduced genuine lexicographical innovations. While few have fallen for the popular belief that Johnson's was "the first dictionary," critics have persistently looked for ways in which Johnson can be called a "first." Sledd and Kolb provided an authoritative answer to many of these questions, arguing that "Johnson, as lexicographer, asked no questions, gave no answers, and invented no techniques which were new to Europe, though they may very well have been new to English lexicography."[8] Still, critics have occasionally turned up respects in which Johnson seems to introduce new practices. Harold B. Allen explores Johnson's originality with respect to usage labels, and Paul Luna notes some genuine innovations in typographic design. Others have explored his influence on his successors, most notably on Noah Webster, Charles Richardson, and the *Oxford English Dictionary*.

Much of the study of the *Dictionary* has been devoted to the illustrative quotations, including Johnson's self-quotations. William Keast and Gwin J. and Ruth Kolb did important early studies of the subject, and investigations of this sort continue to appear at a steady pace in the wake of DeMaria's book. The study of Johnson's sources has provided insight into Johnson's reading, even his world-view. And beginning in the 1980s, the turn to political questions in the wider world of literary studies was

---

7   *Johnson on the English Language*, ix.

8   Sledd and Kolb, *Dr. Johnson's Dictionary*, 4. The passage originally appeared in "Johnson's 'Dictionary' and Lexicographical Tradition," *Modern Philology* 50, no. 3 (1953): 171–194 (at 172).

reflected in a series of studies of the politics of Johnson's *Dictionary*, most of them based on the assumption that the quotations can provide insight into Johnson's politics. This treatment of the quotations has also prompted a backlash among a few critics; in the words of Howard D. Weinbrot, it is not at all clear "What Johnson's Illustrative Quotations Illustrate."

A number of scholars have attempted to extract a "theory of language" from the practice in the *Dictionary*: DeMaria, Rackstraw Downes, and Elizabeth Hedrick have worked to elucidate the theory implicit in Johnson's practice. Others have tried to relate Johnson to other early modern theorists of language, especially John Locke: Roland Hall, Elizabeth Hedrick, James McLaverty, John Middendorf, and Kathleen Wales have all published influential articles on Locke's influence on Johnson's thinking about language.

Another perennial concern is Johnson's place on the prescriptive–descriptive continuum. Johnson wrote frankly in the *Plan* of 1747 about his prescriptive intentions; imagining the English language as "a new world, which it is almost madness to invade," he hoped that he would "at least discover the coast, civilize part of the inhabitants, and make it easy for some other adventurer to proceed farther, to reduce them wholly to subjection, and settle them under laws."[9] By the time he completed his work in 1755, though, he described his obligation "not [to] form, but register the language," and insisted he that he would "not teach men how they should think, but relate how they have hitherto expressed their thoughts."[10] Critics have since argued over the degree to which he hoped to "fix" the language. Randolph Quirk took up the subject in 1974, and Donald Greene, John Barrell, and DeMaria traded a series of letters on the question in the *TLS* in the early 1980s. It has informed many of the general discussions of the *Dictionary* since, and was the subject of a pair of opposed essays by Geoff Barnbrook and Anne McDermott in *Anniversary Essays*. A related question is Johnson's influence, whether intended or not, in "fixing" the language—whether the publication of his *Dictionary* resulted in a standardized orthography or altered the course of semantic shifts. Adam R. Beach, Elizabeth Hedrick, Nicholas Hudson, Geoffrey Hughes take up these questions in essays cited below.

This brief survey touches on only a few of the most important discussions of Johnson's *Dictionary* from 1955 to 2009. Such studies continue to appear at the rate of several dozen a year. Scholarship on the *Dictionary* has in fact become an international phenomenon, with contributions not only from around the Anglophone world but also Europe, India, and East Asia, This bibliography includes several studies from Japan, published both

9   *Johnson on the English Language*, 58.

10   Ibid., 102.

in Japanese and in English. We can only expect that, with reliable and searchable texts of the *Dictionary* available to scholars for the first time, the pace of investigation will quicken yet more. The tercentenary of Johnson's birth, therefore, is unlikely to mark an endpoint of any sort. It does, however, provide a useful opportunity to glance back over the last half-century-plus and to reflect on the most important trends in the study of what may be Johnson's greatest achievement.

Studies of Johnson's *Dictionary*, 1955–2009

ALEXANDER, ROBERT JOHN. "'Empty Sounds': Johnson's *Dictionary* and the Limit of Language." Chapter 3 of "The Diversions of History: A Nonphenomenal Approach to Eighteenth-Century Linguistic Thought." PhD diss., McMaster University, 1999.

ALLEN, HAROLD B. "Samuel Johnson: Originator of Usage Labels." In *Linguistic and Literary Studies in Honor of Archibald A. Hill, IV: Linguistics and Literature; Sociolinguistics and Applied Linguistics*, edited by Mohammed Ali Jazayery, Edgar C. Polome, and Werner Winter, 193–200. The Hague: Mouton, 1979.

ALLEN, JULIA. *Samuel Johnson's Menagerie: The Beastly Lives of Exotic Quadrupeds in the Eighteenth Century*. Banham, Norwich, Norfolk: Erskine Press, 2002.

An exploration of the "exotic quadrupeds" described in the *Dictionary*.

ALLHUSEN, EDWARD, ed. *Fopdoodle and Salmagundi: Words and Meanings from Dr Samuel Johnson's Dictionary That Time Forgot*. Moretonhampstead, Devon: Old House Books, 2007.

Reviews: Claire Harman, "The Words That Time Forgot," *The Telegraph*, 4 October 2007 (with another work); Jane Sullivan, "Of Fizgigs and Jobbernowls," *The Age* (Melbourne), 31 January 2009 (with another work).

ALSTON, ROBIN C. *The English Dictionary*, 30–41, 70–71. Leeds: E. J. Arnold and Son, 1966.

AMORY, HUGH. *Dreams of a Poet Doomed at Last to Wake a Lexicographer*. Cambridge, Mass.: Houghton Library, 1986.

250 copies printed for the Johnsonians.

[ANON.] *A Short-Title Catalog of Eighteenth Century Editions of Dr. Samuel Johnson's "Dictionary" in Special Collections, the Library of the School of Library and Information Science, the University of Western Ontario*. London, Ont.: University of Western Ontario, 1985.

[ANON.] "Johnson's Bestiary." *Transactions of the Johnson Society* (Lichfield) (1997): 24–29.

Humorous piece on *Dictionary* definitions on animals.

[ANON.] "Regulating Language." *The Hindu*, 3 October 2004, 47–48.

ARRIETA, RAFAEL ALBERTO. "El diccionario del Altillo." *La Prensa* (Buenos Aires), 7 August 1960.

In Spanish.

AVIN, I. "Driven to Distinguish: Samuel Johnson's Lexicographic Turn of Mind: A Psychocritical Study." PhD diss., University of St. Andrews, 1997.

BAINBRIDGE, BERYL. "Words Count: Samuel Johnson's Dictionary Was Published 250 Years Ago This Month." *The Guardian*, 2 April 2005, 5.

BALDERSTON, KATHARINE C. "Dr. Johnson's Use of William Law in the Dictionary." *Philological Quarterly* 39 (1960): 379–388.

BANERJEE, A. "Johnson's Patron." *TLS*, 1 June 2007, 17.

A response to Freeman's "Affection's Eye," arguing that the *Dictionary* definitions of *patron* "are quite unexceptionable."

BARNBROOK, GEOFF. "Johnson the Prescriptivist? The Case for the Prosecution." In *Anniversary Essays on Johnson's* Dictionary, edited by Jack Lynch and Anne McDermott, 91–112. Cambridge: Cambridge University Press, 2005.

———. "Usage Notes in Johnson's *Dictionary*." *International Journal of Lexicography* 18, no. 2 (2005): 189–201.

BARRELL, JOHN. "'The Language Properly So-Called': Johnson's Language and Politics." In *English Literature in History, 1730–1780: An Equal, Wide Survey*, 189–205. New York: St. Martin's Press, 1983. Reprinted in *Dr. Johnson and James Boswell*, edited by Harold Bloom, 189–201. New York: Chelsea House Publishers, 1986.

———. Letter to the editor. *TLS*, 10 June 1983, 603.

A response to Donald Greene's letter of 27 May 1983.

BASKER, JAMES G. "Dictionary Johnson amidst the Dons of Sidney: A Chapter in Eighteenth-Century Cambridge History." In *Sidney Sussex College Cambridge: Historical Essays in Commemoration of the Quatercentenary*, edited by D. E. D. Beales and H. B. Nisbet, 131–144. Woodbridge: Boydell Press, 1996.

BATE, WALTER JACKSON. *The Achievement of Samuel Johnson*. New York: Oxford University Press, 1955, 23–25.

———. "Storming the Main Gate: The *Dictionary*." Chapter 15 of *Samuel Johnson*. New York: Harcourt Brace Jovanovich, 1977.

BEACH, ADAM R. "The Creation of a Classical Language in the Eighteenth Century: Standardizing English, Cultural Imperialism, and the Future of the Literary Canon." *Texas Studies in Literature and Language* 43, no. 2 (2001): 117–141.

BELLAMY, LIZ. "The *Dictionary*." Chapter 3 of *Samuel Johnson*. Horndon, Tavistock: Northcote House, 2005.

Bilik, Dorothy. "Johnson Defines an Audience for the *Dictionary.*" *New Rambler: Journal of the Johnson Society of London* 17 (1976): 45–49.

Billi, Mirella. "Johnson's Beauties: The Lexicon of the Aesthetics in the *Dictionary.*" *Textus: English Studies in Italy* 19, no. 1 (2006): 131–150.

Borkowski, David. "(Class)ifying Language: The War of the Word." *Rhetoric Review* 21, no. 4 (October 2002): 357–383.

Boulton, James T., ed. *Johnson: The Critical Heritage.* New York: Barnes & Noble, 1971, entries 13–22 (pages 90–140).

> Reprints Johnson's *Plan*, a notice in the *Bibliothèque raisonée*, Chesterfield's essays in *The World*, two of Johnson's letters, the Preface, Adam Smith's unsigned review in the *Edinburgh Review*, a short selection from John Horne Tooke's *Diversions of Purley*, a review in *Three Philological Essays*, and a letter from Noah Webster.

Brack, O M, Jr., and Robert DeMaria, Jr., eds. *A New Preface by Samuel Johnson: Some Remarks on the Progress of Learning Since the Reformation, Especially with Regard to the Hebrew: Occasion'd by the Perusal of the Rev. Mr. Romaine's Proposal for Reprinting the Dictionary and Concordance of F. Marius de Calasio: With Large Additions and Emendations: In an Address to the Publick by a Stranger to the Editor and a Friend to Learning.* Tempe, Ariz.: Almond Tree Press & Paper Mill, 2001.

Brack, O M, Jr., and Thomas Kaminski. "Johnson, James, and the Medicinal Dictionary." *Modern Philology* 81, no. 4 (May 1984): 378–400.

Braudy, Leo. "Lexicography and Biography in the *Preface* to Johnson's *Dictionary.*" *SEL: Studies in English Literature, 1500–1900* 10, no. 3 (1970): 551–556.

Brewer, Charlotte. "Johnson, Webster, and the *Oxford English Dictionary.*" In *A Companion to the History of the English Language*, edited by Haruko Momma and Michael Matto, 112–121. Malden, Mass.: Wiley-Blackwell, 2008.

> A short overview of three milestone English dictionaries.

Broyard, Anatole. "Johnson's Dictionary." *The New York Times*, 30 August 1981.

Burgess, Anthony. "The Dictionary Makers." *Wilson Quarterly* 17, no. 3 (1993): 104–110.

Burridge, Kate. "'Corruptions of Ignorance,' 'Caprices of Innovation': Linguistic Purism and the Lexicographer." *Johnson Society of Australia Papers* 10 (August 2008): 25–38.

Cacchiani, Silvia. "Desperately, Utterly and Other Intensifiers: On Their Inclusion and Definition in Dr Johnson's *Dictionary.*" *Textus: English Studies in Italy* 19, no. 1 (2006): 217–236.

CAVENDISH, RICHARD. "Publication of Dr Johnson's Dictionary: April 15th, 1755." *History Today* 55, no. 4 (2005): 52–53.

A short notice observing the 250th anniversary of the *Dictionary*.

CHANDRA, NARESH. "Dr. Johnson and the English Language." In *Essays on Dr. Samuel Johnson*, 5–24. Meerut, India: Shalabh, 1986.

CHAPIN, CHESTER. "Samuel Johnson and Joseph Addison's Anti-Jacobite Writings." *Notes and Queries* 48 (March 2001): 38–40.

———. "Samuel Johnson and the Geologists." *Cithara* 42, no. 1 (2002): 33–44.

CLIFFORD, JAMES L. "Dr. Johnson's Dictionary: A Memorable Achievement of the Mind." *The New York Times Book Review*, 10 April 1955, 7. Reprinted in *An Exhibition in Honor of the 200th Anniversary of the Publication of Johnson's Dictionary, 15 April 1755*, 3–6. New York: Columbia University Libraries, 1955.

———. "A Harmless Drudge." Chapter 16 of *Young Sam Johnson*. New York: McGraw-Hill, 1955.

———. "Lexicographer at Work." Chapter 4, and "The *Dictionary*." Chapter 9 of *Dictionary Johnson: The Middle Years of Samuel Johnson*. New York: McGraw-Hill, 1979.

CLINE, EDWARD. "Samuel Johnson: Imperious Lexicographer." *Colonial Williamsburg: The Journal of the Colonial Williamsburg Foundation* 20, no. 1 (1997): 42–48.

COCHRANE, ROBERTSON. "The Man Who Put Words in Their Place: Some of Samuel Johnson's 18th-Century Dictionary Entries Won't Be Found in a Modern Webster's, Such as His Cure for the Bite of a Tarantula: Music." *The Globe and Mail*, 2 October 1993.

COLLINS, H. P. "The Birth of the Dictionary." *History Today* 24 (1974): 197–203.

CONGLETON, J. E. "Johnson's Dictionary, 1755–1955." *South Atlantic Bulletin* 20, no. 4 (1955): 1–4.

———. "Sir Herbert Croft on Revising Johnson's *Dictionary*." *Tennessee Studies in Literature* 13 (1968): 49–62.

———. "Pronunciation in Johnson's Dictionary." In *Papers on Lexicography in Honor of Warren N. Cordell*, edited by J. E. Congleton, J. Edward Gates, and Donald Hobar, 59–81. Terre Haute: Dictionary Society of North America, Indiana State University, 1979.

———. "Callender's Attack on Johnson's Word-List." *Papers of the Dictionary Society of North America* (1981): 25.

———, and ELIZABETH C. CONGLETON. *Johnson's Dictionary: Bibliographical Survey 1746–1984 with Excerpts for All Entries.* Terre Haute: Dictionary Society of North America, 1984.

CONSIDINE, JOHN. "The Lexicographer as Hero: Samuel Johnson and Henri Estienne." *Philological Quarterly* 79, no. 2 (2000): 205–224.

CRAVEN, MAXWELL. "Maxwell Craven" (column). *The Derby Evening Telegraph*, 24 November 2005, 8.

On the 50p coin commemorating the *Dictionary*.

CRYSTAL, DAVID, ed. *Dr Johnson's Dictionary: An Anthology.* London: Penguin Books, 2005.

Reviews: Freya Johnston, "Language and Lingo," *The Sunday Telegraph*, 30 May 2004; Nicholas Lezard, "Bring on the Buffleheaded," *The Guardian*, 16 December 2006, 18; Calum MacDonald, *The Herald* (Glasgow), 12 November 2005, 6 (with other works); John Morrish, *The Independent on Sunday*, 13 November 2005, 18–19 (with other works); Doug Swanson, "Dictionary Anthology a Treasure for Wordsmiths: No Need to Brangle Anymore," *The Edmondton Journal*, 5 February 2006, E11.

DAI, LIULING. "[Some Remarks on Dr. Johnson's English Dictionary]." *Wai guo yu/ Journal of Foreign Languages* 6, no. 34 (1984): 6–9.

In Chinese.

DAVIDSON, J. A. "The Mermaid Inn: Browse along with Dr. Johnson." *The Globe and Mail*, 30 March 1985.

DEAN, TIM. "Psychopoetics of Lexicography: Johnson with Lacan." *Literature and Psychology* 37, no. 4 (1991): 9–28.

DEAN, WILLIAM J. "Here a Word, There a Thousand." *Christian Science Monitor*, 11 June 1986.

DEMARIA, ROBERT, JR. Letter to the editor. *TLS*, 24 June 1983, 667.

———. *Johnson's Dictionary and the Language of Learning.* Chapel Hill: University of North Carolina Press, 1986.

Reviews: N. F. Blake, *Lore and Language* 7, no. 1 (1988): 113–114; Edmund Fuller, "Legacy of a Lexicographer," *The Wall Street Journal*, 23 September 1986; Philip Mahone Griffith, *The Age of Johnson: A Scholarly Annual* 3 (1990): 453–455; Isobel Grundy, *Yearbook of English Studies* 18 (1988): 324–326; Elizabeth Hedrick,

"Reading Johnson's *Dictionary*," *Annals of Scholarship* 7 (1990): 91–101; James McLaverty, *Notes and Queries* 35, no. 2 (1988): 239–241; John H. Middendorf, *Johnsonian News Letter* 46, no. 2 (June 1986–June 1987): 3; Albert Pailler, *Etudes anglaises* 40, no. 2 (1987): 216–217; Murray G. H. Pittock, *British Journal for Eighteenth-Century Studies* 12 (1989): 111–112; Allen Reddick, *Modern Philology* 86, no. 3 (1989): 312–316; Pat Rogers, *London Review of Books* 9, no. 1 (1987): 13–14; Robert Stack, *The Times Higher Education Supplement* 731 (1986): 15; Keith Walker, *TLS*, 30 January 1987, 123; David Womersley, *Review of English Studies* 39, no. 153 (1988): 113–114.

———. "The Theory of Language in Johnson's *Dictionary*." In *Johnson after Two Hundred Years*, edited by Paul J. Korshin, 159–174. Philadelphia: University of Pennsylvania Press, 1986.

———. "The Politics of Johnson's *Dictionary*." *PMLA* 104, no. 1 (1989): 64–74.

———. "Johnson's *Dictionary* and the 'Teutonick' Roots of the English Language." In *Language and Civilization: A Concerted Profusion of Essays and Studies in Honor of Otto Hietsch, I & II*, edited by Claudia Blank and Patrick Selim Huck, 1:20–36. Frankfurt: Peter Lang, 1992.

———. "Johnson's *Dictionary*." Chapter 8 of *The Life of Samuel Johnson: A Critical Biography*. Oxford and Cambridge, Mass.: Blackwell, 1993.

———. "Johnson's *Dictionary*." In *The Cambridge Companion to Samuel Johnson*, edited by Greg Clingham, 85–101. Cambridge: Cambridge University Press, 1997.

———. "Johnson's Extempore History and Grammar of the English Language." In *Anniversary Essays on Johnson's* Dictionary, edited by Jack Lynch and Anne McDermott, 77–91. Cambridge: Cambridge University Press, 2005.

———. "The Gove–Liebert File of Quotations from Johnson's *Dictionary* (II)." *Johnsonian News Letter* 56, no. 1 (2005): 28–30.

On the collection of index cards on which the sources of Johnson's quotations were indexed by Philip Gove and Herman Liebert.

———, ed. *Adam Smith Reviews Samuel Johnson's* "A Dictionary of the English Language." Privately printed for the Johnsonians and the Samuel Johnson Society of Southern California, 2005.

Includes a facsimile of Smith's review in *The Edinburgh Review*.

———. "North and South in Johnson's *Dictionary*." *Textus: English Studies in Italy* 19, no. 1 (2006): 11–32.

———. "Samuel Johnson and the Saxonic Shakespeare." In *Comparative Excellence: New Essays on Shakespeare and Johnson*, edited by Eric Rasmussen and Aaron Santesso, 25–46. New York: AMS Press, 2007.

On Johnson's treatment of Shakespeare in the *Dictionary* in light of his comments on the Germanic origins of the English language.

———, and Gwin J. Kolb. "The Preliminaries to Dr. Johnson's *Dictionary*: Authorial Revisions and the Establishment of the Texts." *Studies in Bibliography* 48 (1995): 121–134.

———, and Gwin J. Kolb. "Johnson's *Dictionary* and Dictionary Johnson." *Yearbook of English Studies* 28 (1998): 19–43.

Dille, Catherine. "The Johnson *Dictionary* Project." *Johnsonian News Letter* 55, no. 2 (2004): 42–44.

———. "The *Dictionary* in Abstract: Johnson's Abridgments of the *Dictionary of the English Language* for the Common Reader." In *Anniversary Essays on Johnson's Dictionary*, edited by Jack Lynch and Anne McDermott, 198–211. Cambridge: Cambridge University Press, 2005.

———. "Johnson's *Dictionary* in the Nineteenth Century: A Legacy in Transition." *The Age of Johnson: A Scholarly Annual* 16 (2005): 21–37.

Doherty, F. M. "Johnson's *Dictionary* and *The Vanity of Human Wishes*: Notes for Readers." *British Journal for Eighteenth-Century Studies* 2 (1979): 206–219.

Dolezal, Fredric F. M. "Charles Richardson's *New Dictionary and Literary Lexicography, Being a Rodomontade upon Illustrative Examples*." *Lexicographica: International Annual for Lexicography* 16 (2000): 104–151.

Downes, Rackstraw. "Johnson's Theory of Language." *Review of English Literature* 3 (October 1962): 29–41.

Eberwein, Robert. "The Astronomer in Johnson's Rasselas." *Michigan Academician: Papers of the Michigan Academy of Science, Arts, and Letters* 5 (1972): 9–15.

Elledge, Scott. "The Naked Science of Language, 1747–1786." In *Studies in Criticism and Aesthetics, 1660–1800: Essays in Honor of Samuel Holt Monk*, edited by Howard Anderson and John S. Shea, 266–295. Minneapolis: University of Minnesota Press, 1967.

Elton, Ben, and Richard Curtis. "Ink and Incapability." Episode 2 of *Blackadder the Third*. Produced by John Lloyd; directed by Mandie Fletcher; written by Ben Elton and Richard Curtis. Aired 24 September 1987.

The Prince Regent (Hugh Laurie) wants to become the patron of Johnson (Robbie Coltrane) for his *Dictionary*. After Baldrick (Tony Robinson) accidentally burns the sole manuscript, Blackadder (Rowan Atkinson) has to recreate the entire thing from scratch. Also includes appearances by a roguish group of poets, including Coleridge (Jim Sweeney), Shelley (Lee Cornes), and Byron (Steve Steen).

An Exhibition in Honor of the 200th Anniversary of the Publication of Johnson's Dictionary, 15 April 1755. Introduction by John R. Turner Ettlinger. New York: Columbia University Libraries, 1955.

Includes James L. Clifford, "Dr. Johnson's Dictionary: A Memorable Achievement of the Mind."

FELSENSTEIN, FRANK. "Some Annotations by Samuel Dyer and Edmund Burke in a Copy of Johnson's 'Dictionary.'" *The Long Room* 18–19 (1979): 27–33.

FERGUS, JAN. "The Provincial Buyers of Johnson's *Dictionary* and Its Alternatives." *The New Rambler*, D:6 (1990–91), 3–5.

FLEEMAN, J. D. "Some of Dr. Johnson's Preparatory Notes for His *Dictionary*, 1755." *Bodleian Library Record* 7, no. 4 (1964): 205–210.

———. "Dr. Johnson's *Dictionary*, 1755." In *Samuel Johnson, 1709–1784: A Bicentenary Exhibition*, edited by Kai Kin Yung, 37–45. London: Arts Council of Great Britain and The Herbert Press, 1984.

———. "Earlier Uses of *Bibliography* and Related Terms." *Notes and Queries* 31 (1984): 30–31.

On the word *bibliographer*.

———. "Johnson's *Dictionary* (1755)." *Trivium* 22 (Summer 1987): 83–88.

———. *The Genesis of Johnson's Dictionary.* Harlow, Essex, England: Longman, 1990.

Part of the Longman facsimile edition of Johnson's *Dictionary of the English Language*.

———. "Johnson in the Schoolroom: George Fulton's Miniature *Dictionary* (1821)." In *An Index of Civilisation: Studies of Printing and Publishing History in Honour of Keith Maslen*, edited by Ross Harvey, Wallace Kirsop, and B. J. McMullin, 163–171. Clayton, Victoria, Australia: Center for Bibliographical and Textual Studies, Monash University, 1993.

———. *A Bibliography of the Works of Samuel Johnson: Treating His Published Works from the Beginnings to 1984.* 2 vols. Oxford: Clarendon Press, 2000, items 47.8PD (1:141–144), 55.4D (1:410–478), 55.4D/A (1:478–483), 56.1DA (1:486–546), 56.1DA/A (1:546–552), 56.1DA/T (1:547–556), 56.1MD (1:556–657).

FLEISSNER, ROBERT F. "*Aroint* and Doctor Samuel Johnson." *Word Watching* 45, no. 3 (1970): 1–3.

FLEMING, LINDSAY. "Johnson, Burton, and Hale." *Notes and Queries* 4 (April 1957): 154.

On the copies of Burton and Hale Johnson used in preparing the *Dictionary*.

FOLKENFLIK, ROBERT. "Samuel Johnson." In *Encyclopædia Britannica*, 15th ed. Chicago: Encyclopædia Britannica, 1995.

Also available through *Encyclopædia Britannica Online*.

———. "The Politics of Johnson's *Dictionary* Revisited." *The Age of Johnson: A Scholarly Annual* 18 (2007): 1–17.

FRASER, MICHAEL. "Chaucer, Johnson, and Shakespeare on CD-ROM." *Computers & Texts* 12 (July 1996): 21–25.

Review essay on Anne McDermott's edition of the *Dictionary* on CD-ROM.

FRITZE, RONALD H. "The Oxford English Dictionary: A Brief History." *Reference Services Review* 17, no. 3 (1989): 61–70.

FUJII, TETSU. "James Boswell Reconstructed from Various Editions of the *Encyclopaedia Britannica*." *The Bulletin of Central Research Institute: Fukuoka University* 116 (1989): 29–60.

———. "How Samuel Johnson Has Been Described in Successive Editions of the *Encyclopaedia Britannica*." *Studies in Eighteenth-Century English Literature*, edited by the Johnson Society of Japan, 71–91. Tokyo: Yusho-Do, 1996.

FULFORD, TIM. "Johnson: The Usurpations of Virility." Chapter 2 of *Landscape, Liberty and Authority: Poetry, Criticism and Politics from Thomson to Wordsworth*. Cambridge: Cambridge University Press, 1996.

On Chesterfield and the *Dictionary*.

FUSSELL, PAUL. "Writing a Dictionary." Chapter 7 of *Samuel Johnson and the Life of Writing*. New York: Norton, 1970.

GEBHARDT, PETER. "Revisiting Dr Johnson." *The Age* (Melbourne), 12 September 2009.

GILMORE, THOMAS B., JR. "Johnson's Attitudes toward French Influence on the English Language." *Modern Philology* 78, no. 3 (1981): 243–260.

———. "Implicit Criticism of Thomson's *Seasons* in Johnson's *Dictionary*." *Modern Philology* 86, no. 3 (1989): 265–273.

GLOVER, STEPHEN L. "'Trumpet' in Samuel Johnson's *A Dictionary of the English Language* (1755)." *ITG [International Trumpet Guild] Journal* 22, no. 4 (1998): 40–43.

GOODE, STEPHEN. "A Generous and Elevated Mind." *Insight on the News* 16, no. 16 (1 May 2000): 4.

On quotations of Johnson in the new *Oxford Dictionary of Quotations*.

GREEN, JONATHON. "Samuel Johnson: The Pivotal Moment." In *Chasing the Sun: Dictionary Makers and the Dictionaries They Made*, 251–283. New York: Henry Holt, 1996.

———. "The Higher Plagiarism." *Critical Quarterly* 44, no. 1 (2002): 97–102.

GREENE, DONALD. Letter to the editor. *TLS*, 27 May 1983, 545.

On Johnson's prescriptiveness.

———. "A Famous Presentation Copy." *The Clark Newsletter* 7 (Fall 1984): 1–2.

On the copy of the Académie Française's *Dictionnaire* presented to Johnson.

———. "The Student of Language and Literature: Lexicographer and Critic." Chapter 7 of *Samuel Johnson*, updated ed. Boston: Twayne, 1989.

GRIFFITH, PHILIP MAHONE. "Dr. Johnson's 'Diction of Common Life' and Swift's *Directions to Servants*." In *Jonathan Swift: Tercentenary Essays*, 266–295. Tulsa: University of Tulsa, 1967.

———. "Samuel Johnson and King Charles the Martyr: Veneration in the *Dictionary*." *The Age of Johnson: A Scholarly Annual* 2 (1989): 235–261.

GROSS, JEFFREY THOMAS. "The Process of Definition in Dr. Johnson's Dictionary: The Poet, Philosopher, and Moralist as Lexicographer." PhD diss., University of Virginia, 1975.

———. "Dr. Johnson's Treatment of English Particles in the *Dictionary*." *University of Mississippi Studies in English* 2 (1981): 71–92.

GROVES, PAUL. "Johnson's Dictionary: Dr Johnson's World in Just 42,773 Words: Dr Samuel Johnson's Dictionary Is 250 Years Old." *Birmingham Post*, 9 April 2005.

GUNN, DANIEL P. "The Lexicographer's Task: Language, Reason, and Idealism in Johnson's *Dictionary* Preface." *The Age of Johnson: A Scholarly Annual* 11 (2000): 105–124.

HAILEY, R. CARTER. "'This Instance Will Not Do': George Steevens and the Revision(s) of Johnson's *Dictionary*." *Studies in Bibliography* 54 (2001): 243–264.

———. "Hidden Quarto Editions of Johnson's *Dictionary*." In *Anniversary Essays on Johnson's* Dictionary, edited by Jack Lynch and Anne McDermott, 228–239. Cambridge: Cambridge University Press, 2005.

HALL, ROLAND. "Locke, Johnson, and the *OED*." *Notes and Queries* 20 (1973): 1–17.

See also comments by Anthony W. Shipps, p. 184.

HAMMONS, DEBORAH. "How Spelling Came to Be." *Christian Science Monitor*, 26 May 1998, 16.

HANCHER, MICHAEL. "Bailey and After: Illustrating Meaning." *Word and Image* 8, no. 1 (1992): 1–20.

HANKS, PATRICK. "Johnson and Modern Lexicography." *International Journal of Lexicography* 18, no. 2 (2005): 243–266.

HARDY, J. P. *"Dictionary" Johnson*. Armidale, N.S.W.: University of New England, 1967.

HARP, RICHARD L., ed. *Dr. Johnson's Critical Vocabulary: A Selection from His* Dictionary. Lanham, MD: University Press of America, 1986.

"The purpose of this book . . . is to put into general circulation those portions of the *Dictionary* that persons interested in literature and writing would find of greatest value."

Reviews: Lionel Basney, *Eighteenth-Century Studies* 21 (Fall 1987): 113–117; John H. Middendorf, *Johnsonian News Letter* 49 (September 1989–June 1990): 22–23; James Rettig, *American Reference Books Annual* 19 (1988): 1074.

HAUSMANN, FRANZ JOSEF. "Samuel Johnson (1709–1784): Bicentenaire de sa mort." *Lexicographica* 1 (1985): 239–242.

In French.

HAWARI, EMMA. "Samuel Johnson and Lessing's Lexicographical Work." *New German Studies* 13, no. 3 (1985): 185–195.

HAYAKAWA, ISAMU. *Jisho hensan no dainamizumu: Jonson, Uebusuta to nihon* ("The Dynamism of Lexicography: Johnson, Webster and Japan"). Tokyo: Jiyusha, 2001.

In Japanese.

HEDRICK, ELIZABETH. "Locke's Theory of Language and Johnson's *Dictionary*." *Eighteenth-Century Studies* 20, no. 4 (1987): 422–444.

———. "Fixing the Language: Johnson, Chesterfield, and *The Plan of a Dictionary*." *ELH* 55, no. 2 (1988): 421–442.

HERZBERG, MAX J. "Johnson Bicentenary." *Word Study* 30 (May 1955): 4–8.

HINES, PHILIP, JR. "George Mason's *Supplement to Johnson's Dictionary* in Manuscript." *Notes and Queries* 27 (1980): 50–55.

HIRST, CHRISTOPHER, and GENEVIEVE ROBERTS. "The A–Z of Johnson's Dictionary: Samuel Johnson Defined Both Language and Life in 18th-Century." *The Independent*, 31 March 2005.

HITCHINGS, HENRY. *Dr Johnson's Dictionary: The Extraordinary Story of the Book that Defined the World*. London: J. Murray, 2005. Published in the United States as *Defining the World: The Extraordinary Story of Dr Johnson's Dictionary*. New York: Farrar, Straus and Giroux, 2005.

A popular overview of the composition of the *Dictionary*, contextualized in SJ's life and the history of lexicography.

Reviews: Nicholas Bagnall, "More than Words," *Literary Review*, April 2005, 45; Christopher Bantick, "Word Wizard's Wonder," *Hobart Mercury*, 9 July 2005, B16; Lisa Berglund, *Dictionaries: Journal of the Dictionary Society of North America* 27 (2006): 184–185; Sarah Burton, "A Treasure House of Words and More," *The Spectator*, 9 April 2005, 37; John Carey, *The Sunday Times*, 27 March 2005 (with another work); Kate Chisholm, "Dr Johnson's Way with Words," *The Sunday Telegraph*, 3 April 2005, 11; Tim Cribb, *South China Morning Post*, 17 April 2005, 5; Jodie Davis, "Words of Wisdom," *The Herald Sun* (Melbourne), 9 July 2005, W29; Kitty Chen Dean, *Library Journal Reviews*, 15 September 2005, 66; Quentin de la Bédoyère, "Setting the Standard," *The Catholic Herald*, 3 June 2005 (with another work); Daniel Dyer, "Defining Story Explores Making of First Solid English Dictionary," *The Cleveland Plain Dealer*, 16 October 2005; Peter Elson, "Defining the Man Who Gave Us the Modern Dictionary: Johnson Could Be Irritable and Rude to His Equals," *The Daily Post* (Liverpool), 6 June 2005, 21; Brian Fallon, "The Life of a Landmark," *The Irish Times*, 7 May 2005, 13; Barbara Fisher, *The Boston Globe*, 2 October 2005, D7; Rosemary Goring, "Great Broth of Words: Dr Johnson's Dictionary Defined the World," *The Herald* (Glasgow), 2 April 2005, 6; William Grimes, "Making a World of Sense, the Long and the Short of It," *The New York Times*, 12 November 2005, B7; Paul Groves, *Birmingham Post*, 9 April 2005, 43–44; Christopher Hawtree, "How to Frighten a Crocodile," *The Independent on Sunday*, 17 April 2005, 32; Christopher Howse, "42,773 Entries, Including Dandiprat, Jobberknowl and Fart: Christopher Howse Celebrates the Life of a Lexicographer Whose Monumental Achievement Nearly Killed Him," *The Daily Telegraph*, 9 April 2005, 7; "It's Only Words," *Aberdeen Press and Journal*, 7 April 2005, 18; Alan Jacobs, "Bran Flakes and Harmless Drudges," *Christianity Today* 12, no. 1 (2006): 23 (with another work); Richard Jenkyns, "Peculiar Words," *Prospect*, 21 April 2005; Peter Kanter, *Johnsonian News Letter* 57, no. 1 (2006): 57–60; Freya Johnston, *The Age of Johnson: A Scholarly Annual* 17 (2006): 417–418; Thomas Keymer, "Meaning Exuberant," *TLS*, 15 April 2005, 10; *Kirkus Reviews*, 15 August 2005; Jeremy Lewis, "A Definitive Guide to

Dr Johnson," *The Mail on Sunday*, 3 April 2005, FB56; Peter Lewis, "Meet the Word Doctor, from A to Z," *The Daily Mail*, 29 April 2005, 60; Roger Lewis, "Tale of the Tome That Gave Us Real Meaning," *The Express*, 1 April 2005, 52; Jack Lynch, *The Washington Examiner*, 17 October 2005; Charles McGrath, "A Man of Many Words: How Dr. Johnson and His Dictionary Helped Discipline an Unruly Language," *The New York Times Book Review*, 4 December 2005, 48–49; Stephen Miller, *Wall Street Journal*, 12 October 2005, D:13; Philip Marchand, "Words, the Daughters of Earth," *The Toronto Star*, 15 January 2006, D6; Andrew Motion, *The Guardian*, 16 April 2005, 13; David Nokes, "The Last Word—Even If Not Adroit," *The Times Higher Education Supplement*, 21 April 2006 (with other works); Andrew O'Hagan, "Word Wizard," *The New York Review of Books* 53, no. 7 (27 April 2006): 12–13; *Publisher's Weekly*, 18 July 2005, 197; Jemma Read, *The Observer*, 24 April 2005, 16; Matthew J. Reisz, *The Independent*, 15 April 2005, 25; David Self, "Colouring in the Words," *The Times Educational Supplement*, 1 April 2005; Will Self, "The First Literary Celebrity," *The New Statesman*, 16 May 2005, 42–44; Jesse Sheidlower, "Defining Moment," *Bookforum* 12, no. 3 (2005): 4–7 (with other works); Tracy Lee Simmons, "Johnson's Canon: On The Trail of the Great Lexicographer," *The Weekly Standard* 11, no. 35 (29 May 2006); Ken Smith, *The Los Angeles Times*, 23 October 2005, R8; James Srodes, *The Washington Times*, 22 January 2006; *The Sunday Mail* (South Australia), 26 June 2005, 79; Paul Tankard, "Let Me Introduce You to Johnson's Dictionary," *Otago Daily Times*, 20–21 August 2005, Weekend Magazine, 8; Ian Thomson, "Fopdoodles, Dandiprats, and Jibes at the Scots," *The Evening Standard*, 18 April 2005, 70; *Time Out*, 1 June 2005, 73; Frank Wilson, "Sparkling Tale of 1st Great English Dictionary," *The Philadelphia Inquirer*, 30 October 2005.

———. "Alphabet Coup: Samuel Johnson Was Motivated by What He Called 'the Exuberance of Signification' in His Mission to Compile the First Comprehensive English Dictionary." *Financial Times Weekend Magazine*, 2 April 2005, 26.

———. "Words Count: Samuel Johnson's Dictionary Was Published 250 Years Ago This Month: Henry Hitchings Reveals Johnson's Technique: An A–Z of English (without the X)." *The Guardian*, 2 April 2005, 5.

———. "Dr Johnson, the Man of Many Words." *BBC History*, April 2005, 44–45.

HOLDER, R. W. "Samuel Johnson, 1709–1784." Chapter 1 of *The Dictionary Men: Their Lives and Times*. Claverton Down, Bath: Bath University Press, 2004.

Includes an engraving by Ignace Joseph de Claussen facing p. 1.

HORGAN, A. D. *Johnson on Language: An Introduction*. Oxford: St. Martin's Press, 1994.

Reviews: Jack Lynch, *Choice* 32 (April 1995): 4345; Anne McDermott, *Review of English Studies* 47, no. 188 (1996): 593–594.

Hudson, Nicholas (Canada). "Johnson's *Dictionary* and the Politics of 'Standard English.'" *Yearbook of English Studies* 28 (1998): 77–93.

———. "Reassessing the Political Context of the *Dictionary*: Johnson and the 'Broad-bottom' Opposition." In *Anniversary Essays on Johnson's Dictionary*, edited by Jack Lynch and Anne McDermott, 61–76. Cambridge: Cambridge University Press, 2005.

Hudson, Nicholas (Australia). "Two Bits of Drudgery: A Homage to Johnson, the Lexicographer." *Johnson Society of Australia Papers*, 2 (1997): 11–15.

———. *Johnson and the* Macquarie: *An Investigation of 250 Years' Progress in Language and Lexicography*. Melbourne: privately printed for the Johnson Society of Australia, 1999.

The David Fleeman Memorial Lecture for 1998.

———. "Mr Johnson Changes Trains." *Johnson Society of Australia Papers* 7 (2005): 65–79.

Hughes, Geoffrey. "Johnson's *Dictionary* and Attempts to 'Fix the Language.'" *English Studies in Africa: A Journal of the Humanities* 28, no. 2 (1985): 99–107.

Hulbert, James Root. *Dictionaries: British and American*. New York: Philosophical Library; London: Andre Deutsch, 1955. Rev. ed., London: Deutsch, 1968, 21–23.

Huntley, Frank L. "Dr. Johnson and Metaphysical Wit; or, *Discordia Concors* Yoked and Balanced." In *Poetic Theory/Poetic Practice*, edited by Robert Scholes, 103–112. Iowa City: Midwest Modern Language Association, 1969.

Iamartino, Giovanni. "Dyer's and Burke's Addenda and Corrigenda to Johnson's *Dictionary* and Clues to Its Contemporary Reception." *Textus: English Studies in Italy* 8, no. 2 (1995): 199–248.

———. "English Flour and Italian Bran: Johnson's *Dictionary* and the Reformation of Italian Lexicography in the Early Nineteenth Century." *Textus: English Studies in Italy* 19, no. 1 (2006): 203–216.

———. "What Johnson Means to Me." *Johnsonian News Letter* 58, no. 1 (March 2007): 18–21.

On the author's fascination with Johnson's *Dictionary* and Barretti's English–Italian dictionary.

———, and Robert DeMaria Jr., eds. "Samuel Johnson's *Dictionary* and the Eighteenth-Century World of Words." Special section in *Textus: English Studies in Italy* 19, no. 1 (2006): 5–261.

Reviews: Elizabeth Hedrick, *Johnsonian News Letter* 59, no. 1 (2008): 55–58.

ILLO, JOHN. "The Polymathic Dictionary." *Western Humanities Review* 18 (Summer 1964): 265–273.

JACKSON, H. J. "Johnson and Burton: The *Anatomy of Melancholy* and the *Dictionary of the English Language*." *English Studies in Canada* 5 (1979): 36–48.

JACKSON, HOWARD. "The Beginnings." Chapter 4 of *Lexicography: An Introduction*. London: Routledge, 2002.

JAIN, NALINI. "Samuel Johnson and Eighteenth Century Ideas of Language." *Rajasthan Studies in English* 17 (1985): 39–52.

JARVIS, SIMON. "Johnson's Authorities: The Professional Scholar and English Texts in Lexicography and Textual Criticism," chapter 6, and "Johnson's Theory and Practice of Shakespearian Textual Criticism," chapter 7 of *Scholars and Gentlemen: Shakespearian Textual Criticism and Representations of Scholarly Labour, 1725–1765*. Oxford: Clarendon Press, 1995.

JENKYNS, RICHARD. "Peculiar Words." *Prospect*, 21 April 2005.

JOHN, VIJAYA. "Johnson's *Dictionary*: Some Reflections." In *Essays on Dr. Samuel Johnson*, edited by T. R. Sharma, 1–4. Meerut, India: Shalabh, 1986.

JOHNSON, NANCY NEWBERRY. "Theories of the Earth in *A Dictionary of the English Language* (1755): Samuel Johnson's Engagement with Early Science." PhD diss., University of Louisiana at Lafayette, 2001.

JOHNSON, SAMUEL. *A Dictionary of the English Language*. 2 vols. New York: AMS Press, 1967.
Facsimile of the first edition.

———. *A Dictionary of the English Language*. Hildesheim: Georg Olms Verlag, 1968.
Facsimile of the first edition.

———. *The Plan of a Dictionary, 1747*. Menston, Yorks.: Scolar Press, 1970.
Facsimile.

———. *A Dictionary of the English Language*. Edited with an introduction by James L. Clifford. Beirut: Librairie du Liban, 1979.
Facsimile of the fourth edition.

———. *A Dictionary of the English Language*. London: Times Books, 1979.
Facsimile of the first edition.

———. *A Dictionary of the English Language*. New York: Arno Press, 1980.
Facsimile of the first edition.

————. *A Dictionary of the English Language.* 2 vols. London: Longman, 1990.
Facsimile of the first edition.

Reviews of this facsimile: Peter Ackroyd, "A Vision of England," *The Times* (London), 22 September 1990; D. J. Enright, *The Independent*, 30 September 1990, 29; Christopher Hawtree, *The Times Educational Supplement*, 3895 (22 February 1991): 35; Gwin J. and Ruth Kolb, *Johnsonian News Letter* 50, no. 3–51, no. 3 (September 1990–September 1991): 6–8; Claude Rawson, "Samuel Johnson Goes Abroad," *London Review of Books* 13, no. 15 (1991): 15–17 (with other works).

————. *Samuel Johnson's Dictionary of the English Language.* Edited by Alexander Chalmers. London: Studio Editions, 1994.

————. *A Dictionary of the English Language Jukyuseiki eigo jiten fukkoku shusei.* Edited by Henry John Todd and Daisuke Nagashima. 4 vols. Tokyo: Yumanishobo, 2001.

————. *A Dictionary of the English Language.* Octavo, 2005.
DVD-ROM or 3 CD-ROM set. Includes an introductory essay by Eric Korn.

Reviews: Robert DeMaria, Jr., *Johnsonian News Letter* 56, no. 2 (September 2005): 58–60; Brian Greene, *Library Journal*, 15 July 2005, 124; Alan Jacobs, "Bran Flakes and Harmless Drudges," *Christianity Today* 12, no. 1 (January–February 2006): 23 (with another work); W. Miller, *Choice* 43 (2005): 0657; Jesse Sheidlower, "Defining Moment," *Bookforum* 12, no. 3 (October–November 2005): 4–7 (with other works).

JOHNSTON, FREYA. "Accumulation in Johnson's *Dictionary.*" *Essays in Criticism: A Quarterly Journal of Criticism* 57, no. 4 (2007): 301–324.

JORDAN, BOB (R. R.). "The Origins and Development of English Dictionaries 1: Early Days: Nathaniel Bailey and Samuel Johnson." *Modern English Teacher* 10, no. 3 (2001): 15–19.

JUNG, SANDRO. "Johnson's *Dictionary* and the Language of William Collins's *Odes on Several Descriptive and Allegoric Subjects.*" *Textus: English Studies in Italy* 19, no. 1 (2006): 69–86.

KAHANE, HENRY, and RENÉE KAHANE. "Dr. Johnson's *Dictionary*: From Classical Learning to the National Language." *Lexicographia* 41 (1992): 50–53.

KEANEY, BRIAN, and BILL LUCAS. "Education: A Short History of Dictionaries—by the Middle of the 18th Century the Chaotic Development of Spoken and Written English Had Prompted Dr Samuel Johnson in England and Noah Webster in America to Compile Dictionaries." *The Guardian*, 14 May 1991.

Keast, William R. "Self-Quotation in Johnson's 'Dictionary.'" *Notes and Queries* 2 (1955): 392–393.

———. "Another Self-Quotation in Johnson's Dictionary." *Notes and Queries* 3 (1956): 262.

———. "The Two *Clarissa*s in Johnson's *Dictionary*." *Studies in Philology* 54 (1957): 429–439.

On Johnson's quotations from *A Collection . . . of Moral and Instructive Sentiments*.

Keenan, Catherine. "Johnson's Defining Glory." *Sydney Morning Herald*, 7 January 2006.

Kennedy, Maev. "New Research Indicates Johnson Gave Up on His Dictionary: Leading Expert Claims that Dr Johnson Abandoned His Dictionary for Several Years—without Telling His Publishers." *The Guardian*, 3 August 2006.

On Anne McDermott's research.

Keogh, Annette Maria. "British Translations: Foreign Languages and Translation in Johnson's *Dictionary*." Chapter 4 of "Found in Translation: Foreign Travel and Linguistic Difference in the Eighteenth Century." PhD diss., Stanford University, 2002.

Kernan, Alvin B. "'The Boundless Chaos of a Living Speech': Johnson and Structural Linguistics." *Princeton Alumni Weekly* 15 (October 1986): 33–38.

———. "Creating an Aura for Literary Texts in Print Culture." Chapter 5 of *Printing Technology, Letters, & Samuel Johnson*. Princeton: Princeton University Press, 1987.

The final section of the chapter, pages 181–203, is titled "Language and the Literary Text: Johnson's *Dictionary*." The book was republished as *Samuel Johnson & the Impact of Print*.

Kezar, Dennis Dean, Jr. "Radical Letters and Male Genealogies in Johnson's *Dictionary*." *SEL* 35, no. 3 (1995): 493–517.

Kirsop, Wallace. "A Note on Johnson's *Dictionary* in Nineteenth-Century Australia and New Zealand." In *An Index of Civilisation: Studies of Printing and Publishing History in Honour of Keith Maslen*, edited by Ross Harvey, Wallace Kirsop, and B. J. McMullin, 172–174. Clayton, Victoria, Australia: Center for Bibliographical and Textual Studies, Monash University, 1993.

Klinkenborg, Verlyn. "Appreciations: Johnson's Dictionary." *The New York Times*, 17 April 2005, section 4, p. 13.

KNOBLAUCH, C. H. "Coherence Betrayed: Samuel Johnson and the 'Prose of the World.'" *Boundary 2: An International Journal of Literature and Culture* 7, no. 2 (1979): 235–260.

KOLB, GWIN J. "Establishing the Text of Dr. Johnson's Plan of a Dictionary of the English Language." In *Eighteenth-Century Studies in Honor of Donald F. Hyde*, edited by W. H. Bond, 81–87. New York: Grolier Club, 1970.

———, ed. *Johnson's Dictionary: Catalogue of a Notable Collection of One Hundred Different Editions of Dr. Johnson's* Dictionary of the English Language, *Some of them Exceedingly Scarce, and All Collected with Great Skill and Industry, Offered for Sale as a Collection*. Dorking: C. C. Kohler, 1986.

———. "Studies of Johnson's *Dictionary*, 1956–1990." *Dictionaries: Journal of the Dictionary Society of North America* 2 (1990): 113–126.

A review essay with commentary on Congleton, DeMaria, Nagashima, and Reddick.

———, and ROBERT DEMARIA, JR. "Dr Johnson's Definition of *Gibberish*." *Notes and Queries* 45, no. 1 (1998): 72–74.

———, and ROBERT DEMARIA, JR., eds. *Johnson on the English Language*. New Haven: Yale University Press, 2005.

The Yale Edition of the Works of Samuel Johnson, vol. 18.

Reviews: O M Brack, Jr., *Johnsonian News Letter* 57, no. 2 (2006): 59–60; H. J. Jackson, *TLS*, 9 December 2005, 29; Frank Kermode, "Lives of Dr. Johnson," *The New York Review of Books* 53, no. 11 (22 June 2006): 28–31 (with other works); Anthony W. Lee, *Modern Philology* 104, no. 4 (May 2007): 529–559 (with other works); Jack Lynch, *Choice* 43, no. 9 (May 2006): 5132; Jack Lynch, "Dr. Johnson Speaks: On Language, English Words, and Life," *The Weekly Standard* 12, no. 16 (1 January 2007); David Nokes, "The Last Word—Even If Not Adroit," *The Times Higher Education Supplement*, 21 April 2006 (with other works); Christopher Ricks, "Dictionary Johnson," *The New Criterion* 24, no. 1 (September 2005): 82–87; Jesse Sheidlower, "Defining Moment," *Bookforum* 12, no. 3 (October–November 2005): 4–7 (with other works); Paul Tankard, *The Southern Johnsonian* 16, no. 57 (March 2009): 2; Victor Wishna, "Words, Words, Words: Two-and-a-Half Centuries after the Publication of Samuel Johnson's Landmark Dictionary, a New Critical Edition Illuminates His Best Intentions," *Humanities* 26, no. 6 (2005): 26–29.

———, and RUTH A. KOLB. "The Selection and Use of the Illustrative Quotations in Dr. Johnson's Dictionary." In *New Aspects of Lexicography: Literary Criticism, Intellectual History, and Social Change*, edited by Howard D. Weinbrot, 61–72. Carbondale and Edwardsville: Southern Illinois University Press; London and Amsterdam: Feffer & Simons, 1972.

————, and JAMES H. SLEDD. "The Reynolds Copy of Johnson's *Dictionary.*" *Bulletin of the John Rylands Library* 37 (March 1955): 446–475.

————, and JAMES H. SLEDD. "The History of the Sneyd-Gimbel and Pigott–British Museum Copies of Dr. Johnson's *Dictionary.*" *Papers of the Bibliographical Society of America* 54 (1960): 286–289.

KORSHIN, PAUL J. "Johnson and Swift: A Study in the Genesis of Literary Opinion." *Philological Quarterly* 48 (1969): 464–478.

————. "The Johnson–Chesterfield Relationship: A New Hypothesis." *PMLA* 85, no. 2 (1970): 247–259.

————. "Johnson and the Renaissance Dictionary." *Journal of the History of Ideas* 35 (1974): 300–312.

————. "Johnson, Samuel (1709–1784)." In *International Encyclopedia of Communications*. Edited by George Gerbner et al. 4 vols. Oxford: Oxford University Press, 1989, 1:371–372.

————. "The Mythology of Johnson's *Dictionary.*" In *Anniversary Essays on Johnson's* Dictionary, edited by Jack Lynch and Anne McDermott, 10–23. Cambridge: Cambridge University Press, 2005.

Korshin demolishes many of the myths and legends that have grown up around the writing of the *Dictionary.*

KURZER, FREDERICK. "Chemistry in the Life of Dr. Samuel Johnson." *Bulletin for the History of Chemistry* 29, no. 2 (2004): 65–88.

Includes appendices: "List of Johnson's Books on Chemistry and Cognate Subjects," "List of Books on Chemistry and Cognate Subjects in the Thrales' Library at Streatham," and "List of Chemical Terms Quoted in Johnson's Dictionary."

LANCASHIRE, IAN. "Dictionaries and Power from Palgrave to Johnson." In *Anniversary Essays on Johnson's* Dictionary, edited by Jack Lynch and Anne McDermott, 24–41. Cambridge: Cambridge University Press, 2005.

————. "Johnson and Seventeenth-Century English Glossographers." *International Journal of Lexicography* 18, no. 2 (2005): 157–171.

LANDAU, SIDNEY I. "A Brief History of English Lexicography." Chapter 2 of *Dictionaries: The Art and Craft of Lexicography.* 2nd ed. Cambridge: Cambridge University Press, 2001.

————. "Johnson's Influence on Webster and Worcester in Early American Lexicography." *International Journal of Lexicography* 18, no. 2 (2005): 217–229.

LAWLESS, JILL. "Samuel Johnson's Dictionary Still a Page-Turner after 250 Years." Associated Press, 21 April 2005.

LEE, ANTHONY W. "Quo Vadis?: Samuel Johnson in the New Millennium." *Modern Philology* 104, no. 4 (2007): 529–559.

> A substantial omnibus review essay on *The Age of Johnson: A Scholarly Annual* 16; Jack Lynch and Anne McDermott, eds., *Anniversary Essays on Johnson's Dictionary*; Howard D. Weinbrot, *Aspects of Samuel Johnson: Essays on His Arts, Mind, Afterlife, and Politics*; O M Brack Jr., ed., *A Commentary on Mr. Pope's Principles of Morality, or Essay on Man*; David Hankins and James J. Caudle, eds., *The General Correspondence of James Boswell, 1757–1763*; Gwin J. Kolb and Robert DeMaria Jr., eds., *Johnson on the English Language*; Roger Lonsdale, ed., *The Lives of the Poets*; Helen Deutsch, *Loving Dr. Johnson*; and Allen Reddick, ed., *Samuel Johnson's Unpublished Revisions to the* Dictionary of the English Language: *A Facsimile Edition.*

LEED, JACOB. "Johnson and Chesterfield: 1746–47." *Studies in Burke and His Time* 12, no. 1 (1970): 1677–1685.

> On the drafting of the *Short Scheme* and the dedication of the *Plan* to Chesterfield.

LEHNERT, MARTIN. "Das english Wörterbuch in Vergangenheit und Gegenwart." *Zeitschrift für Anglistik und Amerikanistik* 4 (1956): 265–323.

> In German.

LERER, SETH. "A Harmless Drudge: Samuel Johnson and the Making of the Dictionary." Chapter 12 of *Inventing English: A Portable History of the Language*. New York: Columbia University Press, 2007.

> An overview of the *Dictionary* in Lerer's account of the history of the language. Includes comments on Johnson's use of Locke and Milton, and the tensions he felt between prescriptive and descriptive linguistics.

LIEBERT, HERMAN W. "Johnson's *Dictionary*, 1755–1955." *Yale Library Gazette* 30 (1955): 27–28.

———. *The Bear and the Phoenix: John Wilkes' Letter on Johnson's Dictionary Newly Printed in Full: With a Note on Johnson and Wilkes*. Privately printed for The Johnsonians, 1978.

LIM, C. S. "Dr Johnson's Quotation from *Macbeth*." *Notes and Queries* 33 (1986): 518.

LIPKING, LAWRENCE. "Man of Letters: *A Dictionary of the English Language*." Chapter 5 of *Samuel Johnson: The Life of an Author*. Cambridge, Mass.: Harvard University Press, 1998.

LITTLEJOHN, DAVID. *Dr. Johnson and Noah Webster: Two Men and Their Dictionaries.* San Francisco: The Book Club of California, 1971.

Reviews: William Kupersmith, *Philological Quarterly* 51 (1972): 707.

LUNA, PAUL. "The Typographic Design of Johnson's *Dictionary.*" In *Anniversary Essays on Johnson's* Dictionary, edited by Jack Lynch and Anne McDermott, 175–197. Cambridge: Cambridge University Press, 2005.

LYNCH, DEIDRE. "'Beating the Track of the Alphabet': Samuel Johnson, Tourism, and the ABCs of Modern Authority." *ELH* 57, no. 2 (Summer 1990): 357–405.

LYNCH, JACK, ed. *Samuel Johnson's Dictionary: Selections from the 1755 Work That Defined the English Language.* Delray Beach, Fla.: Levenger Press, 2002; New York: Walker & Co., 2003; London: Atlantic, 2004.

Reviews: Andrew Billen, "A Work of Harmless Drudgery," *The Times*, 4 December 2004; *Buffalo News*, 24 August 2003, F7; Michael Bundock, *The New Rambler* E:5 (2001–2): 76–77 (with another work); Jeffrey Burke, *Wall Street Journal*, 10 October 2003, W12; John Carey, *The Sunday Times*, 27 March 2005 (with another work); Quentin de la Bédoyère, "Setting the Standard," *The Catholic Herald*, 3 June 2005 (with another work); Janadas Devan, "Word Treat from the Dictionary," *The Straits Times*, (Singapore), 6 June 2004; Jan Freeman, "The Word Zoilist's Delight," *The Boston Globe*, 7 December 2003 (with other works); Bryan A. Garner, "Harmless Drudgery?", *Essays in Criticism* 57, no. 1 (January 2007): 65–72; Jayne Howarth, "Discovering Dictionary Delights the Johnson Way," *Birmingham Post*, 20 November 2004, 53; Christopher Howse, *The Spectator* 20 November 2004, 4848 (with other works); John Izzard, "Messing about in Dictionaries," *Quadrant* June 2005, 85–87; *Johnsonian News Letter* 54, no. 1 (September 2003): 73–74; James J. Kilpatrick, "Hail the Good Dr. Johnson," *The Chicago Sun-Times*, 21 July 2002, 11 (and other papers; syndicated column); Harry Mead, *The Northern Echo*, 1 March 2005, 12; Edward Pearce, "Leave the Gillet, Here's the Kicksey-Wicksey," *The Herald* (Glasgow), 27 November 2004, 7; Michael Potemra, *National Review* 13 October 2003; Jonathan Sale, "Abba and Dr. Johnson," *The Financial Times Weekend Magazine*, 20 November 2004, 29 (with another work); David Self, "Defining Moments in Time," *The Times Educational Supplement*, 29 October 2004, 17; Jesse Sheidlower, "Defining Moment," *Bookforum* 12, no. 3 (2005): 4–7 (with other works); *The Southern Johnsonian* 11, no. 4 (2004): 2; *The Sunday Herald*, 24 October 2004, 1; W. L. Svitavsky, *Choice* 41, no. 3 (2003): 1888; Paul Tankard, "Chapter and Verse" (column), *The Age* (Melbourne), 28 September 2002, "Saturday Extra" 7; David L. Ulin, *The Los Angeles Times*, 9 September 2003, part 2, 13.

———. "Reading Johnson's Unreadable *Dictionary.*" One-hour address, Boston Athenæum, 15 January 2004, broadcast on C-SPAN2's Book TV, 31 January 2004, 8 February 2004, and 22 February 2004.

———. "Johnson's Encyclopedia." In *Anniversary Essays on Johnson's Dictionary,* edited by Jack Lynch and Anne McDermott, 129–146. Cambridge: Cambridge University Press, 2005.

On the boundary between dictionaries, limited to lexical information, and encyclopedias, which are more expansive, and the ways in which SJ's *Dictionary* often crosses the line.

———, ed. *Samuel Johnson's Insults: A Compendium of Snubs, Sneers, Slights, and Effronteries from the Eighteenth-Century Master.* Delray Beach, Fla.: Levenger Press; New York: Walker & Co., 2004. Published in the UK as *Samuel Johnson's Insults: A Compendium of His Finest Snubs, Slights and Effronteries.* London: Atlantic Books, 2005.

An unscholarly collection of insults and put-downs, culled from both the *Dictionary* and SJ's conversation.

Reviews: Lorne Jackson, "Putdowns to Pick Up," *Sunday Mercury,* 30 October 2005, 6; *Johnsonian News Letter* 55, no. 2 (2004): 70; Rob Kyff, *Hartford Courant* (with other works), 22 June 2004, D2; D. Murali, "Elevate the Insult to an Art Form," *The Hindu Business Times,* 6 November 2005; Bill Ott, "The Age of Insults," *Booklist,* 1 April 2004; Michael Pakenham, *The Baltimore Sun,* 6 June 2004, 8F; *Publisher's Weekly,* 26 January 2004, 169; Elissa Schappell, *Vogue* 526 (June 2004): 90 (with other works); Paul Tankard, "Insulting Words in Johnson's Dictionary," *The Southern Johnsonian* 13, no. 48 (August 2006): 8; *Western Daily Press* (Bristol), 24 December 2005, 34.

———. "Dr. Johnson's Revolution." *The New York Times,* 2 July 2005, A15. OpEd. Reprinted as "Samuel Johnson: Words for a New Nation." In *The International Herald Tribune,* 5 July 2005, 9.

An Op-Ed essay on the importance of SJ's *Dictionary* in early America, including SJ's principles of selection.

———. "Enchaining Syllables, Lashing the Wind: Samuel Johnson Lays Down the Law." Chapter 4 of *The Lexicographer's Dilemma: The Evolution of "Proper" English, from Shakespeare to "South Park."* New York: Walker & Co., 2009.

On debates over descriptive and prescriptive lexicography, and Johnson's debt to the tradition of the common law.

———, and ANNE MCDERMOTT, eds. *Anniversary Essays on Johnson's Dictionary.* Cambridge: Cambridge University Press, 2005.

Fourteen original scholarly essays on previously neglected areas of the Dictionary.

Reviews: *Contemporary Review* October 2005 (with other works); Elizabeth Hedrick, *Johnsonian News Letter* 57, no. 1 (2006): 51–55; Werner Hüllen, *Historiographia Linguistica* 33, no. 3 (2006): 426–430; H. J. Jackson, "Big and Little Matters: Discrepancies in the Genius of Samuel Johnson," *TLS,* 11

November 2005, 3–4 (with other works); Frank Kermode, "Lives of Dr. Johnson," *The New York Review of Books* 53, no. 11 (22 June 2006): 28–31 (with other works); A[nthony] W. Lee, *Choice* 43, no. 7 (March 2006): 3876; Anthony W. Lee, *Modern Philology* 104, no. 4 (2007): 529–559 (with other works); Lynda Mugglestone, *Notes and Queries* 53 (2006): 560–563 (with another work); David Nokes, "The Last Word—Even If Not Adroit," *The Times Higher Education Supplement* 1739 (21 April 2006), 22 (with other works); Chris P. Pearce, "'Gleaned as Industry Should Find, or Chance Should Offer It': Johnson's *Dictionary* after 250 Years," *The Age of Johnson: A Scholarly Annual* 17 (2006): 341–362.

McAdam, E. L., Jr. "Inkhorn Words before Dr. Johnson." In *Eighteenth-Century Studies in Honor of Donald F. Hyde*, edited by W. H. Bond, 187–206. New York: Grolier Club, 1970.

———, and George Milne, eds. *Johnson's Dictionary: A Modern Selection*. New York: Pantheon, 1963.

Reviews: Emma Hagestadt and Christopher Hirst, *The Independent*, 13 July 1996; John Mullan, *The Guardian*, 1 December 1995.

McCaffery, Stephen. "Prior to Meaning: The Protosemantic and Poetics." PhD diss., SUNY Buffalo, 1998.

Includes a section on the theories of language implicit in the *Dictionary*.

McCoshan, Duncan ("Knife"). "Publication Day for Johnson's Dictionary." *The New Statesman*, 1 August 1997, 37. Reprinted in *Transactions of the Johnson Society* [Lichfield] (1997): 48.

Cartoon.

McCracken, David. "The Drudgery of Defining: Johnson's Debt to Bailey's *Dictionarium Britannicum*." *Modern Philology* 66, no. 4 (1969): 338–341.

McDavid, Virginia. "Dictionary Labels for Usage Levels and Dialects." *Papers on Lexicography in Honor of Warren N. Cordell*, 1979, 21–36. Terre Haute: Dictionary Society of North America, Indiana State University.

McDermott, Anne. "Johnson's Use of Shakespeare in the Dictionary." *The New Rambler* D:5 (1989–1990), 7–16.

———. "A Corpus of Source Texts for Johnson's *Dictionary*." *Corpora across the Centuries: Proceedings of the First International Colloquium on English Diachronic Corpora*, edited by Merja Kytö, Matti Rissanen and Susan Wright, 151–154. Amsterdam and Atlanta: Rodopi, 1994.

———. "The Reynolds Copy of Johnson's *Dictionary*: A Re-Examination." *Bulletin of the John Rylands University Library of Manchester* 74, no. 1 (1992): 29–38.

―――. "The Defining Language: Johnson's *Dictionary* and *Macbeth.*" *Review of English Studies* 44, no. 176 (November 1993): 521–538.

―――. "The Intertextual Web of Johnson's *Dictionary* and the Concept of Authorship." In *Early Dictionary Databases*, edited by Ian Lancashire and T. Russon Wooldridge, 165–172. CCH Working Papers 4. Toronto: University of Toronto, 1994. Reprinted in *Publications de l'Institut national de la langue française: Dictionairique et lexicographie* vol. 3, *Informatique et dictionnaires anciens* (1995), edited by Bernard Quemada, 165–171.

―――. "Textual Transformations: The *Memoirs of Martinus Scriblerus* in Johnson's *Dictionary.*" *Studies in Bibliography* 48 (1995): 133–148.

―――. "The Making of Johnson's *Dictionary* on CD-ROM." *Transactions of the Johnson Society* (Lichfield), (1995–96): 29–37.

―――. "Preparing the *Dictionary* for CD-ROM." *The New Rambler* D:12 (1996–97): 17–25.

―――, ed. *A Dictionary of the English Language on CD-ROM.* Cambridge: Cambridge University Press, 1996.

CD-ROM for Windows or Macintosh, containing a full transcription and page images for the first and fourth editions, except for the front matter.

Reviews: Jenni Ameghino, *The Birmingham Evening Post*, 23 March 1996; *Book World* 27 (5 October 1997): 15; J. C. D. Clark, *History Today* 46 (December 1996): 55, and 46 (12 February 1997): 48; Robert Folkenflik, "Samuel Johnson: The Return of the Jacobites and Other Topics," *Eighteenth-Century Studies* 33, no. 2 (Winter 2000): 289–299 (with other works); *Indexer* 20 (October 1996): 109; Hugh John, *The Times Educational Supplement*, 26 April 1996; Mark Kohn, *The Independent*, 31 March 1996, 40; C. LaGuardia and E. Tallent, *Library Journal*, 122, no. 8 (1 May 1997): 148; Jack Lynch, *Choice* 34, no. 7 (March 1997): 1155; Jack Lynch, *The Age of Johnson: A Scholarly Annual* 9 (1998): 352–357; Jim McCue, *The Times*, 21 June 1996, Features; John Naughton, *The Observer*, 24 March 1996, 16; G. W. Pigman, *Huntington Library Quarterly* 61, no. 1 (1998): 115–126 (with other works); Charmaine Spencer, *The Independent*, 20 May 1996, 15; Michael Suarez, "English Engine for Sense and Meaning," *The Times Higher Education Supplement*, 12 July 1996, Multimedia, 12.

―――. "Johnson's *Dictionary* and the Canon: Authors and Authority." *The Yearbook of English Studies* 28 (1998): 44–65.

―――. "Samuel Johnson, *Dictionary.*" In *A Companion to Literature from Milton to Blake*, edited by David Womersley, 353–359. Oxford: Blackwell, 2000.

———. "Creating an Electronic Edition of Johnson's *Dictionary*: Developments of Solutions to Some Problems." In *Standards und Methoden der Volltextdigitalisierung*, edited by Thomas Burch, Johannes Fournier, Kurt Grtner, and Andrea Rapp, 153–160. Mainz: Akademie der Wissenschaften und der Literatur, 2003.

———. "Johnson the Prescriptivist? The Case for the Defense." In *Anniversary Essays on Johnson's* Dictionary, edited by Jack Lynch and Anne McDermott, 113–128. Cambridge: Cambridge University Press, 2005.

———. "Johnson's Definitions of Technical Terms and the Absence of Illustrations." *International Journal of Lexicography* 18, no. 2 (2005): 173–187.

———. "The Compilation Methods of Johnson's *Dictionary*." *The Age of Johnson: A Scholarly Annual* 16 (2005): 1–20.

———. "Johnson's Editing of Shakespeare in the *Dictionary*." In *Comparative Excellence: New Essays on Shakespeare and Johnson*, edited by Eric Rasmussen and Aaron Santesso, 115–138. New York: AMS Press, 2007.

"Lexicography and textual criticism were . . . reciprocal activities and both were part of a larger project to purify the English language, to set it on a par with the languages of France and Italy as exhibited in their great national lexicons, and by a parallel to present Shakespeare as a great national writer."

———, and MARCUS WALSH. "Editing Johnson's *Dictionary*: Some Editorial and Textual Considerations." In *The Theory and Practices of Text-Editing: Essays in Honour of James T. Boulton*, edited by Ian Small and Marcus Walsh, 35–61. Cambridge: Cambridge University Press, 1991.

MCENROE, NATASHA. "Defining the English Language." *Language Magazine* 2, no. 9 (2003): 24–25.

MCINNIS, RAYMOND G. "Discursive Communities/Interpretive Communities: The New Logic, John Locke and Dictionary-Making, 1660–1760." *Social Epistemology* 10, no. 1 (1987): 107–122.

MACK, RUTH. "The Historicity of Johnson's Lexicographer." *Representations* 76 (Fall 2001): 61–87.

———. "The Historicity of Johnson's Lexicographer." Chapter 2 of "Literary Historicity: Literary Form and Historical Thinking in Mid-Eighteenth-Century England." PhD diss., Johns Hopkins University, 2003.

———. "Too Personal? Teaching the Preface." *Johnsonian News Letter* 57, no. 1 (2006): 9–13.

McLaverty, James. "From Definition to Explanation: Locke's Influence on Johnson's *Dictionary*." *Journal of the History of Ideas* 47, no. 3 (1986): 377–394.

McManis, Sam. "Attitude: What Samuel Johnson Had in Abundance." *The News Tribune* (Tacoma), 8 May 2005.

A brief introduction to the *Dictionary*.

Martin, Peter. "A Lifeline: The *Dictionary*." Chapter 14 of *Samuel Johnson: A Biography*. Cambridge, Mass.: The Belknap Press of Harvard University Press, 2008.

Masi, Silvia. "Lexicographic Material under Observation: From Johnson's *Dictionary* to a Model for a Cognition-Based Dictionary of Lexical Patterns." *Textus: English Studies in Italy* 19, no. 1 (2006): 237–258.

Mason, H. A. "Johnson and Dryden on 'Bacchanalian.'" *Notes and Queries* 31 (1984): 397.

Johnson uses the word *bacchanalian* in *Rambler* 71, but it does not appear in the *Dictionary*.

Matthews, Jack. "The Dictionary: The Poetry of Definitions." *Antioch Review* 51, no. 2 (1993): 294–300.

Merrell, James H. "Johnson and Boswell on National Public Radio." *Johnsonian News Letter* 55, no. 2 (2004): 19–20.

Two pieces from "Writer's Almanack" read by Garrison Keillor, on the anniversary of Boswell's meeting with Johnson and the anniversary of the *Dictionary*'s publication.

Middendorf, John H. "Ideas vs. Words: Johnson, Locke, and the Edition of Shakespeare." In *English Writers of the Eighteenth Century*, edited by John H. Middendorf et al, 249–272. New York: Columbia University Press, 1971.

Miller, Robert Carroll. "Johnson's Dictionary Categorized: A Selection for Eighteenth-Century Studies." PhD diss., Texas A&M University, 1975.

Misenheimer, James B., Jr., and Robert K. O'Neill. "The Cordell Collection of Dictionaries and Johnson's Lexicographic Presence: The Love of Books in Two Centuries." *The New Rambler* C:24 (1983): 33–47.

Mitchell, Linda C. "Johnson among the Early Modern Grammarians." *International Journal of Lexicography* 18, no. 2 (2005): 203–216.

Miyoshi, Kasujiro. "Priestley no eibunten to Johnson no eigojiten." *The Journal of Okayama Women's Junior College* 10 (1987): 49–57.

"Priestley's *Rudiments* and Johnson's *Dictionary*." In Japanese.

———. "Johnson no jiten: Yourei no gogakushiteki igi." *The Journal of Okayama Women's Junior College* 12 (1989): 125–133.

"Johnson's *Dictionary*: The Linguistic Significance of Its Citations." In Japanese.

———. *Johnson's and Webster's Verbal Examples: With Special Reference to Exemplifying Usage in Dictionary Entries.* Tübingen: Max Niemeyer Verlag, 2007.

An extensive comparative study of Johnson's and Webster's use of examples, with much of the evidence drawn from the letter *L* in both dictionaries.

MORGENTALER, GOLDIE. "Johnson, the Lexicographer: Just a Drudge?" *The Gazette* (Montreal), 8 June 1996.

MORRISON, RICHARD. "A Man of Many Words (Including Jobbernowl)." *The Times* (London), 15 April 2005, T2, T5.

MUGGLESTONE, LYNDA. "Departures and Returns: Writing the English Dictionary in the Eighteenth and Nineteenth Centuries." In *The Victorians and the Eighteenth Century: Reassessing the Tradition,* edited by Francis O'Gorman and Katherine Turner, 144–162. Aldershot: Ashgate, 2004.

MULLAN, JOHN. "The Rise of Mr Nobody: Dr Johnson Had No Trouble Defining the Word Failure." *The Guardian,* 6 March 1999.

NAGASHIMA, DAISUKE. "Johnson's Dictionary Reconsidered." *Studies in English Literature* (Tokyo) 41 (1964): 35–57.

———. "An Historical Assessment of Johnson's Dictionary." *Anglica* 6, no. 1–2 (1966): 161–200.

———. "The Mutual Debt between Johnson and Lowth." *Studies in English Literature* (Tokyo) 44, no. 2 (1968): 221–232.

On the treatment of grammar.

———. "Backgrounds of Dr. Johnson's *Dictionary*." *Studies in the Foreign Languages and Literature* 4 (1968): 123–156.

———. "Johnson as an English Grammarian." *Studies in the Foreign Languages and Literature* 5 (1969): 177–200.

———. *Johnson no Eigo Jiten: Sono Rekishiteki Igi.* Tokyo: Taishukan, 1983.

"Johnson's *Dictionary*: Its Historical Significance." In Japanese.

———. "Jisho Hensansha, Gogakusha to shite no Johnson." *Eigo Seinen* 130 (1984): 428–429.

On Johnson as lexicographer and philologist.

———. "A Note on Dr. Johnson's *History of the English Language*." In *Linguistics across Historical and Geographical Boundaries: In Honour of Jacek Fisiak on the Occasion of His Fiftieth Birthday*. 2 vols. Edited by Dieter Kastovsky and Aleksander Szwedek, 1:525–531. Berlin: Mouton de Gruyter, 1986.

———. "Johnson's Use of Skinner and Junius." In *Fresh Reflections on Samuel Johnson: Essays in Criticism*, edited by Prem Nath, 283–298. Troy: Whitston, 1987.

———. *Johnson the Philologist*. Hirakata: Intercultural Research Institute, Kansai University of Foreign Studies, 1988.

———. "Jonson no Eigojiten shinkenkyu" (A new study of Johnson's *Dictionary* [by Allen Reddick]), *Eigo Seinen (The Rising Generation)* 137, no. 3 (1991): 138–139. In Japanese.

———. "Samuel Johnson: The Road to the *Dictionary*." *Studies in English Literature* (Japan), 72 (1995): 63–75.

———. "How Johnson Read Hale's *Origination* for His *Dictionary*: A Linguistic View." *The Age of Johnson: A Scholarly Annual* 7 (1996): 247–298.

———. "Johnson's Revisions of His Etymologies." *Yearbook of English Studies* 28 (1998): 94–105.

———. "The Biblical Quotations in Johnson's *Dictionary*." *The Age of Johnson: A Scholarly Annual* 10 (1999): 89–126.

———. "Dr Johnson's *Dictionary*: A Philological Survey." *Bulletin of Koshien University College of Humanities* 4:C (2000): 1–22.

———. "Two Pen-and-Ink Inscriptions on Copies of Johnson's *Dictionary* in Japan." *Johnsonian News Letter* 56, no. 2 (2005): 36–38.

NAKAHARO, AKIO. "Johnson no 'Jisho' to Shakespeare no Inyoku." *Eigo Seinen* 120 (1974): 263–264. On the quotations. In Japanese.

NEWNHAM, DAVID. "The Outsider: Play it Again, Sam: David Newnham Visits the Rose-Red City where Dr Johnson, Lexicographer and Clever-Clogs Learnt His Letters." *The Guardian*, 31 July 1999, Travel, 9.

NICHOL, DON. "The Big English Dictionary at 250: Some of Samuel Johnson's Definitions Had a Twist to Them; Others Were Just Plain Wrong." *The Globe and Mail*, 15 April 2005, A14.

NICHOLLS, GRAHAM. "Johnson Reads for the *Dictionary*." *The New Rambler* E:3 (1999–2000): 29–34.

Nokes, David. "A Harmless Drudge," chapter 6, and "The *Dictionary*," chapter 8, of *Samuel Johnson: A Life.* London: Faber and Faber, 2009.

Noyes, Gertrude E. "The Critical Reception of Johnson's *Dictionary* in the Latter Eighteenth Century." *Modern Philology* 52 (February 1955): 175–191.

O'Kill, Brian. *The Lexicographic Achievement of Johnson.* Harlow, Essex, England: Longman, 1990.

Part of the Longman facsimile edition of Johnson's *Dictionary of the English Language.*

Ormsby, Eric. "The Boundless Chaos of a Living Speech." *The New York Sun,* 16 November 2005.

Országh, Laszlo. "Johnson Lexikográfai Modszere." *Filológiai Közlöny* 2 (1956): 251–265.

In Hungarian, with summaries in Russian and English on p. 339.

Osselton, Noel E. "Formal and Informal Spelling in the 18th Century." *English Studies* 44 (August 1963): 267–275.

———. "Dr. Johnson and the English Phrasal Verb." In *Lexicography: An Emerging International Profession,* edited by R. Ilson, 7–16. Manchester: Manchester University Press, 1986.

———. "Alphabetisation in Monolingual Dictionaries to Johnson." *Exeter Linguistic Studies* 14 (1989): 165–173.

———. "Dr. Johnson and the Spelling of Dispatch." *International Journal of Lexicography* 7, no. 4 (1994): 307.

———. "Phrasal Verbs: Dr. Johnson's Use of Bilingual Sources." In *Chosen Words: Past and Present Problems for Dictionary Makers,* 93–103. Exeter: University of Exeter Press, 1995.

A lightly revised reprint of "Dr. Johnson and the English Phrasal Verb," above.

———. "Hyphenated Compounds in Johnson's *Dictionary*." In *Anniversary Essays on Johnson's* Dictionary, edited by Jack Lynch and Anne McDermott, 160–174. Cambridge: Cambridge University Press, 2005.

———. "Usage Guidance in Early Dictionaries of English." *International Journal of Lexicography* 19, no. 1 (2006): 99–105.

Pearce, Christopher P. "Terms of Corruption: Samuel Johnson's *Dictionary* in Its Contexts." PhD diss., University of Texas, 2004.

Reviews: Robert DeMaria, Jr., *Johnsonian News Letter* 56, no. 1 (2005): 46–47.

———. "Johnson's Proud Folio: The Material and Rhetorical Contexts of Johnson's Preface to the *Dictionary*." *The Age of Johnson: A Scholarly Annual* 15 (2004): 1–35.

———. "The Pleasures of Polysemy: A Plan for Teaching Johnson's *Dictionary of the English Language* in an Eighteenth-Century Course." *Johnsonian News Letter* 56, no. 2 (2005): 10–14.

———. "Recovering the 'Rigour of Interpretative Lexicography': Border Crossings in Johnson's *Dictionary*." *Textus: English Studies in Italy* 19, no. 1 (2006): 33–50.

PINNAVAIA, LAURA. "Idiomatic Expressions Regarding Food and Drink in Johnson's *Dictionary of the English Language* (1755 and 1773)." *Textus: English Studies in Italy* 19, no. 1 (2006): 151–166.

PIREDDU, SILVIA. "The 'Landscape of the Body': The Language of Medicine in Johnson's *Dictionary*." *Textus: English Studies in Italy* 19, no. 1 (2006): 107–130.

POTKAY, ADAM. "Johnson and the Terms of Succession." *SEL: Studies in English Literature, 1500–1900* 26, no. 3 (1986): 497–509.

QUIRK, RANDOLPH. "A Glimpse of Eighteenth-Century Prescriptivism." In Quirk, *The Linguist and the English Language*, 37–45. New York: St. Martin's Press, 1974.

RAWSON, C. J. "Johnson's Bibliothèque." *Notes and Queries* 7 (February 1960): 71.

On the definition of *bibliothèque*.

REDDICK, ALLEN H. "Hopes Raised for Johnson: An Example of Misleading Descriptive and Analytical Bibliography." *TEXT: Transactions of the Society for Textual Scholarship* 2 (1985): 245–249.

———. "The Making of Johnson's *Dictionary* 1746–55 and 1771–73." PhD diss., Columbia University, 1985.

———. *The Making of Johnson's Dictionary, 1746–1773*. Cambridge: Cambridge University Press, 1990. Rev. ed., 1996.

Reviews: David R. Anderson, *South Atlantic Review* 58, no. 3 (1993): 116–118; Paula Backscheider, *SEL: Studies in English Literature, 1500–1900* 31 (1991): 569–614 (with other works); Janet Barron, *The Times Higher Education Supplement*, 18 January 1991; Nicholas A. Basbanes, *Worcester Telegram and Gazette*, Datebook, 24 February 1991, 17; W. B. Carnochan, "Johnson's Human Monument," *TLS*, 19 April 1991, 9–10; George Allan Cate, *Papers of the Bibliographical Society of America* 84 (1990): 440–441; Paul Clayton, *Notes and Queries* 39 (June 1992): 231–232; Robert DeMaria, *Modern Philology* 90 (1992): 268–273; James Gray, *Dalhousie Review* 70 (Summer 1990): 260–263; Christopher Hawtree, "Definitions of Value," *The Times Educational Supplement*, 22 February 1991 (with another work); Elizabeth Hedrick, *Johnsonian News Letter* 50, no. 3–51, no. 3 (September 1990–September 1991): 5–6; Verlyn Klinkenborg, *Harvard Book Review* 19–20 (Winter–Spring 1991): 17; Paul J. Korshin, *The Age of Johnson: A Scholarly Annual* 4 (1991): 417–424; Anne McDermott, *British Journal for Eighteenth-Century Studies*, 17, no. 1 (1994): 74–79; Claude Rawson, "Samuel Johnson Goes Abroad," *London Review of Books* 13, no. 15 (1991): 15–17 (with other works); Pat Rogers, *Review of English Studies* 45 (May 1994): 259–260; G. Scholtz, *Choice* 28, no. 9 (1991): 4972; Michael Steckel, *Libraries and Culture* 29 (1994): 233–235; Michael F. Suarez, *Eighteenth-Century Studies* 26 (Spring 1993): 514–517; Robert Taylor, *Boston Globe*, 31 December 1990; Laurence Urdang, *Verbatim* 20, no. 2 (1993): 8–10 (with another work); Robert Ziegler, *Papers on Language & Literature* 28 (Fall 1992): 457–475.

———. *Johnson's "Dictionary": The Sneyd-Gimbel Copy*. Cambridge, Mass.: Privately printed for the Johnsonians, 1991. Correcting slips bound in and pasted onto pages. 250 copies printed.

———. "Teaching the *Dictionary*." In *Approaches to Teaching the Works of Samuel Johnson*, edited by David R. Anderson and Gwin J. Kolb, 84–91. New York: MLA, 1993.

———. "Johnson beyond Jacobitism: Signs of Polemic in the *Dictionary* and the *Life of Milton*." *ELH* 64, no. 4 (1997): 983–1005.

———. "Johnson's *Dictionary of the English Language* and Its Texts: Quotation, Context, Anti-Thematics." *Yearbook of English Studies* 28 (1998): 66–76.

———. "Dictionaries." In *Encyclopedia of the Enlightenment*. Edited by Alan Kors. 4 vols., 1:352–356. Oxford: Oxford University Press, 2003.

———. "Revision and the Limits of Collaboration: Hands and Texts in Johnson's *Dictionary*." In *Anniversary Essays on Johnson's* Dictionary, edited by Jack Lynch and Anne McDermott, 212–227. Cambridge: Cambridge University Press, 2005.

———, ed. *Samuel Johnson's Unpublished Revisions to the* Dictionary of the English Language: *A Facsimile Edition*. Cambridge: Cambridge University Press, 2005. **Reviews:** Susan Carlile, *Eighteenth-Century Book Reviews Online*, 17 August 2009; Robert DeMaria, Jr., *Johnsonian News Letter* 57, no. 1 (2006): 60–62; H. J. Jackson, "Big and Little Matters: Discrepancies in the Genius of Samuel Johnson," *TLS*, 11 November 2005, 3–4 (with other works); Frank Kermode, "Lives of Dr. Johnson," *The New York Review of Books* 53, no. 11 (22 June 2006): 28–31 (with other works); Anthony W. Lee, *Modern Philology* 104, no. 4 (2007): 529–559 (with other works); James McLaverty, *The New Rambler* E:8 (2004–5): 13–21; Lynda Mugglestone, *Notes and Queries* 53 (December 2006): 560–563 (with another work); David Nokes, "The Last Word—Even If Not Adroit,"

The Times Higher Education Supplement, 21 April 2006 (with other works); Shef Rogers, *Papers of the Bibliographical Society of America* 101, no. 2 (2007): 247–248; Cynthia Wall, *SEL: Studies in English Literature, 1500–1900* 46 (2006): 657–724 (with other works).

———. "Le Dictionnaire de la langue anglaise de Samuel Johnson." In *Les Dictionnaires en Europe au XVIIIe siècle*, edited by Marie Leca-Tsiomis, a special issue of *Revue Dix-huitième siècle* 38 (2006): 225–235.

In French.

———. "Johnson and Richardson." In *The Oxford History of English Lexicography*. Edited by A. P. Cowie, 2 vols., 1:154–181. Oxford: Clarendon Press, 2009.

A careful account of Johnson's *Dictionary* and Charles Richardson's *New Dictionary of the English Language*, which "provocatively illuminates aspects of Johnson's works." Includes illustrations.

REED, JOSEPH W., JR. "Noah Webster's Debt to Samuel Johnson." *American Speech: A Quarterly of Linguistic Usage* 37, no. 2 (1962): 95–105.

REID, S. W. "Charles Brockden Brown's Copy of Johnson's Dictionary (1783)." *Serif* 11, no. 4 (1975): 12–20.

RIVARA, ANNIE. "Savoir délirant et encyclopédie détraquée: Figures de savant fou dans le *Prince Rasselas* de Johnson et le *Compère Mathieu* de Du Laurens." In *Folies romanesques au siècle des lumières*, edited by René Démoris and Henri Lafon, 351–364. Paris: Desjonquères, 1998.

In French.

ROGERS, PAT. "Johnson's Lives of the Poets and the Biographic Dictionaries." *Review of English Studies* 31, no. 122 (May 1980): 149–171.

———. "Language and Literature." Chapter 6 of *Johnson*. Oxford: Oxford University Press, 1993.

ROTHSCHILD, LOREN R. *Johnson's Dictionary: Being an Account of Certain Facts concerning Its Author; Method of Preparation; Significance; and Containing References to Various Interesting Definitions and an Attempt to Relate Certain Aspects of That Great Work to the Contemporary Philological Debate*. Pacific Palisades: Rasselas Press, 1984.

———. *Samuel Johnson's Dictionary: A Lecture Presented at the Huntington Library May 27, 2009 on the Occasion of the Opening of the Exhibition "Samuel Johnson: Literary Giant of the Eighteenth Century."* Los Angeles: The Samuel Johnson Society of the West, 2009.

A keepsake of Rothschild's wide-ranging introduction to the *Dictionary* to mark the opening of the Huntington's exhibition in 2009.

Ruml, Treadwell, II. "The Younger Johnson's Texts of Pope." *Review of English Studies* 36, no. 142 (May 1985): 180–198.

On the editions of Pope used in the *Dictionary*.

Russell, Terence M. "Architecture and the Lexicographers: Three Studies in Eighteenth-Century Publications, pt. 3: Samuel Johnson and *A Dictionary of the English Language*." *Edinburgh Architecture Research* 22 (1995): 59–79.

———, ed. *The Encyclopaedic Dictionary in the Eighteenth Century: Architecture, Arts and Crafts*. Vol. 4: *Samuel Johnson: A Dictionary of the English Language*. Brookfield, Vt.: Ashgate Press, 1997.

Examines 700 *Dictionary* entries on architecture.

Reviews: B. Arcistewska, *Journal of the Society of Architectural Historians* 58, no. 1 (1999): 79–82; A. Gomme, *TLS*, 6 February 1998, 10; D. C. Chambers, *Albion* 30, no. 4 (1998): 695–698.

Ruxin, Paul. "Synonymy and Satire by Association." *The Caxtonian* 14, no. 5 (May 2006): 1–5. Reprinted in *Johnsonian News Letter* 58, no. 2 (2007): 34–41.

On Boswell's inscribed copy of John MacLaurin's *Essays in Verse*, including the poem "On Johnson's Dictionary" (reproduced here).

Samuel Johnson: The Dictionary Man. Directed by Richard Alwyn. BBC Four. Aired 26–27 June 2006.

One-hour television documentary.

San Juan, E., Jr. "The Actual and the Ideal in the Making of Samuel Johnson's Dictionary." *University of Toronto Quarterly* 34 (1965): 146–158.

Scanlan, J. T. "Johnson's *Dictionary* and Legal Dictionaries." *Textus: English Studies in Italy* 19, no. 1 (2006): 87–106.

Schreyer, Rudiger. "Illustrations of Authority: Quotations in Samuel Johnson's *Dictionary of the English Language* (1755)." *Lexicographica: International Annual for Lexicography* 16 (2000): 58–103.

Sharma, Mahanand. "Dr. Johnson and Babu Shyam Sunder Dass as Lexicographers." In *Essays on Dr. Samuel Johnson*, edited by T. R. Sharma, 75–84. Meerut, India: Shalabh, 1986.

Shapiro, Fred R. "Samuel Johnson's Usage of the Word *Literary*." *American Notes and Queries* 21 (1983): 70.

Sherbo, Arthur. "1773: The Year of Revision." *Eighteenth-Century Studies* 7 (1973): 18–39.

On the revision to the *Dictionary* and the Shakespeare edition.

———. "Nil Nisi Bonum: Samuel Johnson in the *Gentleman's Magazine*, 1785–1800." *College Literature* 16, no. 2 (1989): 168–181.

SIEBERT, DONALD T. "*Bubbled, Bamboozled*, and *Bit*: 'Low Bad' Words in Johnson's *Dictionary*." *SEL: Studies in English Literature, 1500–1900* 26, no. 3 (1986): 485–496.

SILVA, PENNY. "Johnson and the *OED*." *International Journal of Lexicography* 18, no. 2 (2005): 231–242.

SIMON, IRÈNE. "Poets, Lexicographers, and Critics." *Cahiers de l'Institut de linguistique de Louvain* 17, no. 1–3 (1991): 163–179.

SIMPSON, JOHN. "What Johnson Means to Me." *Johnsonian News Letter* 56, no. 1 (2005): 6–7.

SLEDD, JAMES. "The Lexicographer's Uneasy Chair." *College English* 23 (1962): 682–683.

Relating *Webster's Third New International* to Johnson's *Dictionary*.

———, and GWIN J. KOLB. *Dr. Johnson's Dictionary: Essays in the Biography of a Book*. Chicago: University of Chicago Press, 1955.

Reviews: J. C. Bryce, *Review of English Studies*, n.s. 9 (1958): 219–220; Donald J. Greene, *JEGP* 55 (1956): 331–334; D. T. Starnes, *MLN* 71 (1956): 309–311; W. K. Wimsatt, Jr., *Philological Quarterly* 35 (1956): 308–310.

SMITH, GILES. "Johnson: The Gardener of Chaos: Giles Smith on the Roots of the Modern Dictionary, and the OED's Debt to the Presiding Genius of Samuel Johnson." *The Independent*, 1 April 1989.

SMITH, JAMES W. "A History of the Dictionary of English Usage to 1900." PhD diss., University of Texas at Austin, 1971.

———. "A Sketch of the History of the Dictionary of English Usage." In *Papers on Lexicography in Honor of Warren N. Cordell*, edited by J. E. Congleton, J. Edward Gates, and Donald Hobar, 47–58. Terre Haute: Dictionary Society of North America, Indiana State University, 1979.

SMITH, TIMOTHY WILSON. "The Making of Dictionary Johnson (1745–1755)." Chapter [3] of *Samuel Johnson*. London: Haus, 2004.

SORENSEN, JANET. "'A Grammarian's Regard to the Genius of Our Tongue': Johnson's *Dictionary*, Imperial Grammar, and the Customary National Language." Chapter 2 in her *Grammar of Empire in Eighteenth-Century British Writing*, 63–103. Cambridge: Cambridge University Press, 2000.

STEIN, GABRIELE. "Word-Formation in Dr. Johnson's *Dictionary of the English Language*." *Dictionaries: Journal of the Dictionary Society of North America* 6 (1985): 66–112.

STONE, JOHN. "Seventeenth-Century Jurisprudence and Eighteenth-Century Lexicography: Sources for Johnson's Notion of Authority." *SEDERI* 7 (1996): 79–92.

———. "John Cowell's Interpreter: Legal Tradition and Lexicographical Innovation." *SEDERI* 10 (1999): 121–129.

———. "Law and the Politics of Johnson's *Dictionary*." *The European English Messenger* 12, no. 1 (2003): 54–58.

———. "The Law, the Alphabet, and Samuel Johnson." In *Anniversary Essays on Johnson's* Dictionary, edited by Jack Lynch and Anne McDermott, 147–159. Cambridge: Cambridge University Press, 2005.

STUPIN, L. P. "Slovari S. Dzhonsona (1755) i N. Uebstera (1828) kak vyrazhenie idei predpisyvaiushohego slovaria" ["The Dictionaries of S. Johnson (1755) and N. Webster (1828) as an Expression of the Idea of a Dictionary as Precept"], *Vestnik Leningradskogo universiteta: Seriia istoriia, iazyk, literatura* 3 (1976): 122–127.

A consideration of the authoritarian tendencies in both dictionaries. In Russian with an English summary.

SUDAN, RAJANI. "Lost in Lexicography: Legitimating Cultural Identity in Johnson's *Preface* to the *Dictionary*." *The Eighteenth Century: Theory and Interpretation* 39, no. 2 (1998): 127–146.

———. "Institutionalizing Xenophobia: Johnson's Project." Chapter 1 of *Fair Exotics: Xenophobic Subjects in English Literature, 1720–1850* (Philadelphia: University of Pennsylvania Press, 2002.

SUWABE, HITOSHI. "On Samuel Johnson's Definition of 'Oats.'" *Review of the Faculty (Humanities and Social Science Section) of the* [Tokyo] *Electro-Communications University* (1977).

TAKAYANAGI, SHUN'ICHI. "'Copious without Order, Energetick without Rules'— Dr Johnson and the Present State of Japanese: Reflections on the New Nihon Kokugo Dai-Jiten." *Monumenta Nipponica* 32, no. 1 (1977): 75–86.

TALUKDAR, SUDIP. "Dr. Johnson's Extraordinary Venture: *The Dictionary*." In *Essays on Dr. Samuel Johnson*, edited by T. R. Sharma, 51–57. Meerut, India: Shalabh, 1986.

TANKARD, PAUL. "Contexts for Johnson's *Dictionary*." *Genre* 35, no. 2 (2003): 253–282.

THOMAS, EUGENE J. "A Bibliographical and Critical Analysis of Johnson's *Dictionary*, with Special Reference to Twentieth Century Scholarship." PhD diss., University of Wales, 1974.

———. "Dr. Johnson and His Amanuenses." *Transactions of the Johnson Society* (Lichfield) (1974): 20–30.

———. "From Marginalia to Microfiche." In *The Computer and Literary and Linguistic Studies*, edited by Alan Jones and R. F. Churchhouse, 293–296. Cardiff: University of Wales Press, 1976.

TIEKEN-BOON VAN OSTADE, INGRID. "Dr. Johnson and the Auxiliary Do." *Hiroshima Studies in English Language and Literature* 33 (1988): 22–39.

———. "Dr Johnson and the Auxiliary DO." *Folia Linguistica Historica* 10, no. 1–2 (1989): 145–162.

TILLOTSON, GEOFFREY. "Johnson's Dictionary." *Spectator*, 29 April 1955, 527–528. Reprinted in Tillotson, *Augustan Studies*, 224–228. London: Athlone Press, 1961.

TODD, WILLIAM B. "Variants in Johnson's *Dictionary*, 1755." *Book Collector* 14 (Summer 1965): 212–213.

———. "Leigh Hunt's Annotations in Johnson's Dictionary." *Modern Philology* 73, no. 4 (Supplement) (May 1976): S110–112.

TRAUTMANN, THOMAS R. "Dr. Johnson and the Pandits: Imagining the Perfect Dictionary in Colonial Madras." *Indian Economic and Social History Review* 38, no. 4 (2001): 374–397. Reprinted in *Land, Politics, and Trade in South Asia*, edited by Sanjay Subrahmanyam, 186–215. New Delhi and New York: Oxford University Press, 2004.

TUCKER, SUSIE I. "Dr. Watts Looks at the Language." *Notes and Queries* 6 (1959): 274–79.

On Johnson's debt to Isaac Watts.

———. "'Forsooth, Madam.'" *Notes and Queries* 9 (1962): 15–16.

On the definition of *forsooth*.

———. "Dr. Johnson Misread?" *Notes and Queries* 12 (June 1965): 146–158.

On the word *immaculate*.

TURNAGE, MAXINE. "Samuel Johnson's Criticism of the Works of Edmund Spenser." *SEL: Studies in English Literature, 1500–1900* 10, no. 3 (1970): 557–567.

VANCIL, DAVID. "Some Observations about the Samuel Johnson Miniature Dictionaries in the Cordell Collection." *Textus: English Studies in Italy* 19, no. 1 (2006): 167–178.

VRIES, CATHARINA MARIA DE. *In the Tracks of a Lexicographer: Secondary Documentation in Samuel Johnson's Dictionary of the English Language (1755).* Leiden: Led, 1994.

WAIN, JOHN. "Diversions of a Lexicographer." Chapter 11 of *Samuel Johnson.* New York: McGraw-Hill, 1974.

WALES, KATHLEEN. "Johnson's Use of Synonyms in Dictionary and Prose Style: The Influence of John Locke?" *Prose Studies* 8, no. 1 (1985): 25–34.

WALKER, IAN C. "Dr. Johnson and *The Weekly Magazine.*" *Review of English Studies* 19, no. 73 (1968): 14–24.

WALKER, KEITH. "Some Notes on the Treatment of Dryden in Johnson's *Dictionary.*" *Yearbook of English Studies* 28 (1998): 106–109.

WECHSELBLATT, MARTIN. "The Pathos of Example: Professionalism and Colonialization in Johnson's Preface to the *Dictionary.*" *The Yale Journal of Criticism* 9, no. 2 (1996): 381–403.

WEINBROT, HOWARD D. "Johnson's Dictionary and *The World*: The Papers of Lord Chesterfield and Richard Owen Cambridge." *Philological Quarterly* 50 (1971): 663–669.

———. "Samuel Johnson's *Plan* and the Preface to the *Dictionary*: The Growth of a Lexicographer's Mind." In *New Aspects of Lexicography: Literary Criticism, Intellectual History, and Social Change*, edited by Howard D. Weinbrot, 73–94. Carbondale and Edwardsville: Southern Illinois University Press; London and Amsterdam: Feffer & Simons, 1972. Reprinted in *Aspects of Samuel Johnson: Essays on His Arts, Mind, Afterlife, and Politics*, 29–52. Newark: University of Delaware Press, 2005.

———. "What Johnson's Illustrative Quotations Illustrate: Language and Viewpoint in the *Dictionary.*" In *Anniversary Essays on Johnson's Dictionary*, edited by Jack Lynch and Anne McDermott, 46–60. Cambridge: Cambridge University Press, 2005. Reprinted in *Aspects of Samuel Johnson: Essays on His Arts, Mind, Afterlife, and Politics*, 53–71. Newark: University of Delaware Press, 2005.

WELLS, RONALD A. "The Authoritarian Tradition in Language: England." Chapter 2 of *Dictionaries and the Authoritarian Tradition.* The Hague: Mouton, 1973.

The final two sections of the chapter. "The Dictionary as Authority: Samuel Johnson" (40–43) and "The Reception of Johnson's *Dictionary*" (43–47), consider Johnson's place in the prescriptive–descriptive continuum.

WILDERMUTH, MARK E. "Samuel Johnson and the Aesthetics of Complex Dynamics." *The Eighteenth Century: Theory and Interpretation* 48, no. 1 (2007): 45–60.

Wildermuth works "in the wake of postmodernism, to contextualize Johnson's double focus on order and disorder, on universal global norms and localized deviance—at least with particular regard to his literary criticism and lexicography, wherein we find his most lucid discussion of an uncertainty principle informing his epistemology and aesthetics."

WILENTZ, AMY. "Mr. Los Angeles, Samuel Johnson." *The Los Angeles Times*, 7 June 2009, A28.

"Johnson, I concluded, could have lived happily in Los Angeles. . . . Johnson's dictionary was his era's Wikipedia, its Google, and Johnson himself was the 18th century equivalent of a blogger."

WILSON, BEE. "Defining Tastes." *The New Statesman* 12, no. 500 (9 April 1999): 40–41.

On definitions of foods in the *Dictionary*.

WILSON, ROSS. "The Dictionary and Drink." *New Rambler: Journal of the Johnson Society of London* C6 (1969): 24–43.

WIMSATT, WILLIAM K., JR. "Johnson's Dictionary: April 15, 1955." In *New Light on Dr. Johnson: Essays on the Occasion of His 250th Birthday*, edited by Frederick W. Hilles, 65–90. New Haven: Yale University Press, 1959.

Includes a facsimile from Bacon's *Essays* with Johnson's annotations.

———. "Johnson's Dictionary." In Wimsatt, *The Day of the Leopards: Essays in Defense of Poems*, 162–180. New Haven: Yale University Press, 1976.

WOOD, NIGEL. "Johnson's Revisions to His *Dictionary*." *The New Rambler* D:3 (1987–1988), 23–28.

———. "'The Tract and Tenor of the Sentence': Conversing, Connection, and Johnson's *Dictionary*." *Yearbook of English Studies* 28 (1998): 110–127.

WOODHOUSE, J. R. "Dr. Johnson and the *Accademia della Crusca*: A Conjunction of Anniversaries." *Notes and Queries* 32 (1985): 3–6.

WOODMAN, THOMAS. "Language." Chapter 8 of *A Preface to Samuel Johnson*. London and New York: Longman, 1993.

YARDLEY, JONATHAN. "Amazingly Enough, the First Great Dictionary was Basically the Work of One Man." *The Washington Post*, 13 November 2005, T5.

Contributors

THOMAS A. HORROCKS is Associate Librarian of Houghton Library for Collections. He received his PhD in history from the University of Pennsylvania, where he focused on early American history, the history of the book in American culture, and the history of medicine in early America. He is the author of *Popular Print and Popular Medicine: Almanacs and Health Advice in Early America* (2008), and editor of *A Monument More Durable than Brass: The Donald & Mary Hyde Collection of Dr. Samuel Johnson* (2009). Co-editor of *The Living Lincoln* (2011), a book of essays on Abraham Lincoln, he is currently writing a biography of James Buchanan.

HOWARD D. WEINBROT is Ricardo Quintana Professor of English and William Freeman Vilas Research Professor in the College of Letters and Science, University of Wisconsin, Madison. His latest books are *Menippean Satire Reconsidered: From Antiquity to the Eighteenth Century* (2005) and *Aspects of Samuel Johnson* (2005). He is currently finishing a book entitled *Literature, Religion, and the Evolution of Culture, 1660–1780*.

JAMES G. BASKER is the Richard Gilder Professor of Literary History at Barnard College, Columbia University, and President of the Gilder Lehrman Institute of American History. His publications include *Amazing Grace: An Anthology of Poems about Slavery 1660–1810* (2002) and *Early American Abolitionists: A Collection of Anti-Slavery Writings 1760–1820* (2005). His scholarly edition of *Roderick Random* is forthcoming in 2012 for the Georgia Edition of the Works of Tobias Smollett. He is currently writing a book provisionally entitled *Samuel Johnson, Abolitionist: The Story Boswell Never Told*.

JAMES ENGELL is Gurney Professor of English and professor of comparative literature at Harvard University, where he served as chair of the Department of English from 2004 to 2010. Author and editor of numerous books on eighteenth- and nineteenth-century literature and criticism, current issues in higher education, and environmental studies, he has published several articles and book chapters on Johnson, edited *Johnson and His Age* (1984), and is a member of the editorial committee of the Yale Edition of the Works of Samuel Johnson. Among his regular course offerings are ones covering all genres of eighteenth-century British literature.

NICHOLAS HUDSON, professor of English at the University of British Columbia, is the author of two books on Johnson, *Samuel Johnson and Eighteenth-Century Thought* (1988) and *Samuel Johnson and the Making of Modern England* (2003). He has also written *Writing and European Thought, 1660–1830* (1994), co-edited (with Aaron Santesso) *Swift's Travels: Eighteenth-Century British Satire and its Legacy* (2009), and published numerous essays on eighteenth-century thought and culture. He is currently completing a new book, *A Long Revolution: Social Hierarchy and Literary Change, 1660–1832*.

JACK LYNCH is professor of English at Rutgers University in Newark, New Jersey. He is the author of *The Age of Elizabeth in the Age of Johnson* (2002) and *Deception and Detection in Eighteenth-Century Britain* (2008), and editor of *The Age of Johnson: A Scholarly Annual*. He is now editing *Samuel Johnson in Context* for Cambridge University Press.

ALLEN REDDICK is professor of English literature at the University of Zürich. His publications on Samuel Johnson include *The Making of Johnson's Dictionary 1746–1773* (2nd. rev. ed., 1996) and *Samuel Johnson's Unpublished Revisions to His Dictionary of the English Language* (2005). His current research involves the description and analysis of books distributed throughout the world by the eighteenth-century republican Thomas Hollis in support of "liberty" causes.

Johnson After Three Centuries:
New Light on Texts and Contexts

Johnson After Three Centuries: New Light on Texts and Contexts examines several aspects of Johnson's career through fresh perspectives and original interpretations by some of the best-known and widely-respected scholars of our time. Edited by Thomas A. Horrocks and Howard D. Weinbrot, the volume includes essays by James G. Basker, James Engell, Nicholas Hudson, Jack Lynch, and Allen Reddick.

THOMAS A. HORROCKS is Associate Librarian of Houghton Library for Collections. He is the author of *Popular Print and Popular Medicine: Almanacs and Health Advice in Early America* (2008) and *Harvard's Lincoln* (2009), and editor of *A Monument More Durable Than Brass: The Donald & Mary Hyde Collection of Dr. Samuel Johnson* (2009). Co-editor of *The Living Lincoln* (2011), a book of essays on Abraham Lincoln, he is currently writing a biography of James Buchanan.

HOWARD D. WEINBROT is Ricardo Quintana Professor of English and William Freeman Vilas Research Professor in the College of Arts and Letters and Science, University of Wisconsin, Madison. His latest books are *Menippean Satire Reconsidered: From Antiquity to the Eighteenth Century* (2005) and *Aspects of Samuel Johnson* (2005). He is currently finishing a book entitled *Literature, Religion, and the Evolution of Culture, 1660–1780*.

COVER ILLUSTRATION: Josiah Wedgwood & Sons. *Samuel Johnson.* 1784. Jasperware. *2003JM-214.

ISBN 9780981885841

Houghton Library of the Harvard College Library

Cambridge, Massachusetts